Handbook for Pre-school SEN Provision

The **Code of Practice** in relation to the Early Years

Second Edition

Collette Drifte

 David Fulton Publishers

David Fulton Publishers Ltd
The Chiswick Centre, 414 Chiswick High Road, London W4 5TF

www.fultonpublishers.co.uk

First published in 1998 in Great Britain by David Fulton Publishers 2003

Second edition 2003

10 9 8 7 6 5 4 3 2

David Fulton Publishers is a division of Granada Learning, part of ITV plc.

British Library Cataloguing in Publication Data
A catalogue record for this book is available from the British Library.

ISBN 1-85346-837-1

Designed and typeset by Kenneth Burnley, Wirral, Cheshire
Printed and bound in Great Britain by Thanet Press, Margate

Contents

Introduction

The legislative basis

In January 2002, the revised *Special Educational Needs (SEN) Code of Practice* came into operation with the implementation of the *Special Educational Needs and Disability Act 2001*. The new Act retained the strengths and positive elements of the original *SEN Code of Practice*, while simultaneously introducing further aspects to ensure better and more inclusive provision for children who have special educational needs.

January 2002 – how did we reach this point?

In order to make sense of the updated legislation, it is useful and important to examine the legal framework leading up to the 2001 Act, since a historical overview of special educational needs and disability legislation puts into perspective the rights of the child and the responsibilities of the adults involved with the child.

Pre-1978

Disabled children were placed in segregated schools, institutions or hospitals, usually according to a perceived disability or degree of learning difficulty, often with labels we would not tolerate today. Terms such as 'asylum', 'mental school', 'cretin', 'mongol', 'handicapped' or 'crippled' were in common use.

1978–1981

In 1978, the *Warnock Report* was published, leading to the implementation of *The Education Act (1981)*, which recognised that a child's difficulties are interactive and contextual, that is they are not within the child and needing 'treatment'. The Act was a watershed and began the process that has brought us to today's position.

1989

The Children Act was passed and required, among other things, the identification of and provision for disabled children, particularly those under the age of eight. It was another extremely important act because for the first time, disabled children were included in the wider framework of legal powers, duties and protections relating to all children. Local Education Authorities and Social Services are obliged under this Act to provide various services for disabled children.

1993

The Education Act (1993) repealed the 1981 act, but retained and strengthened its core principles and included an SEN tribunal to enable parental rights of appeal. The main philosophy of providing entitlements for the child was kept in this Act, and parental involvement and empowerment began to have more of a focus.

1994

The first version of the *SEN Code of Practice* came into effect and provided a guideline for the implementation of the 1993 *Education Act*. It ensured a standardised framework for providing appropriate and individualised education for children with special needs, and meant that wherever a child lived or moved to, the services should be continuous.

1995

The Disability Discrimination Act came into force and clarified disabled people's rights of employment, obtaining goods and services, buying or renting property or land, and transport. Under this Act, a person is termed 'disabled' if they have a physical or mental impairment that has a substantial and long-term adverse effect on their ability to carry out normal daily activities. Education was exempt from this Act, including most early years settings, except as providers of goods and services. After the 1997 General Election, however, the new Labour government consulted the Disability Rights Task Force on how education could be included in disability discrimination duties, specifically in protecting pupils (and potential pupils) from discrimination on the grounds of their disability.

Since 1996, the *social* care of young children in private, voluntary and statutory providers of early years services that are not classed as schools, has been covered by this act, but education and schools did not come under its umbrella until 2001.

1996

With the passing of *The Nursery Education and Grant Maintained Schools Act* in 1996, all early years providers were required to 'have due regard to' the *SEN Code of Practice*. This meant that nursery schools and other maintained settings had to make appropriate provision for the children who had special educational needs in their care. Greater rights were granted to parents, the duties of schools were tightened up and the regulations for assessing children and issuing Statements of Special Educational Needs were made more specific, such as putting in place time limits for the process.

1998

The SEN Action Plan, which followed the Green Paper *Excellence for All Children* (1997) was put into place, with a strong emphasis on inclusion, parent partnership and multi-agency collaboration. At this stage, the term 'integration' was widely used among professionals, but 'inclusion' as a concept was becoming the norm. (For more discussion on the difference between integration and inclusion, see page 2) The *Action Plan* stressed the importance of the holistic approach, with an acknowledgement that working in partnership with parents and other agencies is the way forward.

2001

The Special Educational Needs and Disability Act finally addressed the educational provision that was excluded from the 1995 *Disability Discrimination Act. All* early years providers now have a duty not to discriminate against a disabled child in the education and day care or other services provision that they offer, on the grounds of the child's disability. They have an obligation to implement the *SEN Code of Practice* and they should put in place strategies to make sure their setting is fully inclusive.

The purpose of the handbook

The main purpose of this book is to help all early years providers put into place a structure within their setting that implements the recommendations of the new *SEN Code of Practice*. 'Early years providers' means all settings and establishments offering educational and/or care provision for children under statutory school age. The book offers practical suggestions for ways to plan and implement a framework that ensures, in general terms, an inclusive policy, and more specifically, a logical and easy-to-follow path through the stages of the *Code of Practice*, from early identification to statutory assessment for a Statement of Special Educational Needs.

By following the guidelines in the book, staff in early years settings will be able to formulate a clear and workable SEN policy leading to practices which are fully inclusive and user-friendly. They will be able to produce a portfolio that can be used to illustrate their policies and practices to agents such as Ofsted who may require evidence of the setting's commitment to the *Code of Practice*.

The structure

The different sections

The handbook is divided into five parts, guiding the reader through the whole of the identification and assessment process. Each part is designed to be freestanding and independent of the others, although necessarily closely linked, in order that the reader can immediately access the required information without having to read the entire book.

Part 1 explores the revised *SEN Code of Practice* and what it means for early years practitioners in terms of new or revised responsibilities and requirements. It examines the distinction between integration and inclusion, the concept of differentiation and some important aspects of SEN policy-making.

Part 2 deals with the early stages of expressing concern about a child, including the identification of various potential difficulties. It includes appropriate photocopiable forms for recording staff's concerns.

Part 3 looks at the first formal stage of the *Code of Practice*, Early Years Action. It discusses the roles and responsibilities of the various professionals involved and describes the progression to the next stage. Again, it includes appropriate photocopiable forms.

Part 4 moves on to the next stage of the *Code*, Early Years Action Plus. Roles and responsibilities of practitioners are explored, including the involvement of relevant outside agencies, and a further set of photocopiable forms provides a resource for the setting's SEN records.

Part 5 offers strategies for going through the process of Statutory Assessment possibly leading to the issue of a Statement of Special Educational Needs. While most local education authorities (LEAs) have their own standard forms, this section has similar photocopiable forms that can be used as guidelines for completing other official and/or obligatory forms that an LEA may require from a setting.

The photocopiable forms

These can be used by practitioners in any pre-school setting, and are intended to be flexible. They can be adapted and redesigned in order to make them more customised, or they can be used as they stand if they are appropriate to a particular establishment. They have sections that may not be needed at a specific point in the child's progress and so practitioners should not feel that completion of every part is obligatory – they will know best what is appropriate at each stage. It is important for practitioners to be aware, however, that some or all of the information recorded on the forms at an earlier stage of identification and/or assessment may be used as part of the body of evidence gathered for later stages, including statutory assessment.

Further reading

Finally, there is a section at the back of the book with suggestions for further reading. All of the recommended texts have been selected because of their very practical nature and their accessible style. The DES/DfES documents have also been listed in this section and, while some readers may find them less 'reader-friendly' than the other recommended texts, they are nevertheless the core part of the whole process and serve as essential reference material.

PART 1

The revised *SEN Code of Practice* and practitioners in early years settings

After the original *SEN Code of Practice* had been in operation for several years, practitioners were consulted by the government on ways to improve the practicalities of making it work, and the outcome was the revised *Code of Practice* that was implemented from January 2002. It incorporated several fundamental and important changes, among which were:

- the five original stages leading to the issuing of a Statement of Special Educational Needs being replaced by three levels;
- children in *all* early years provision to be included in the legislation;
- a greater emphasis on the involvement of both the child and the parents;
- new rights of appeal for parents;
- a reduction of the paperwork involved;
- Individual Education Plans (IEPs) to focus only on what is *additional to* and *different from* the rest of the curriculum.

The five stages leading to the issuing of a Statement of Special Educational Needs being replaced by three levels

The revised *Code of Practice* simplified the process, going from identification of a difficulty to the issuing of a Statement of Special Educational Needs. The original five stages were replaced by three levels: Early Years Action (or School Action), Early Years Action Plus (or School Action Plus) and Statutory Assessment.

Early Years Action replaced the original Stages 1 and 2, and deals with the early identification of a difficulty, and methods of dealing with it in-house. Early Years Action Plus replaced Stage 3, and incorporated the involvement of outside agencies or specialists, while Statutory Assessment replaced Stages 4 and 5, possibly leading to the writing of a Statement of Special Educational Needs.

The three levels are discussed in depth in Parts 3, 4 and 5 of this book.

The inclusion of children in *all* early years provision

'All early years provision' means all pre-school settings, whether maintained, voluntary or private, that offer early years education; local authority day care providers such as day nurseries or family centres; registered playgroups and pre-school groups; registered childminding networks and local authority Portage schemes. These settings have to write an SEN policy, designate a Special Educational Needs Coordinator (SENCO), adopt the recommendations of the *Code of Practice*, train staff to identify and work with children who have special educational needs, and link up with the local provision of services and support.

Inclusion is fast becoming an automatic part of the planning that goes on in early years settings. There still remains some confusion, however, about the difference between inclusion and integration, and indeed the terms continue to be used interchangeably by many people, although in fact they do not mean the same thing. From the earliest days of special educational needs legislation, 'integration' was the buzzword, and schools were eager to promote their ideas for integrating children with special needs into their settings. Over the following two decades there has been a gradual and almost subtle change in the best way of working to support these children, and the philosophy of inclusion has developed from this.

Inclusion or integration – what is the difference?

- *Integration* means placing children with special educational needs in a mainstream setting and expecting them to change in order to 'fit in'; integration does not encourage the changes in attitude necessary at institutional and individual levels, to enable the children to participate as fully as possible in what is on offer; *the onus is on the child to change*.

- *Inclusion* means placing the children in a mainstream setting and ensuring that the attitudes, policies and practices at institutional and individual levels enable the children to participate as fully as possible; *the onus is on the setting and everybody involved in it to change, if necessary*.

Young children are not in a position to ensure by themselves that they are included, so it is our responsibility as both adults and practitioners to make this happen.

What are the benefits of inclusion for children with special needs and their families?

- Children with SEN benefit from contact with peers of all abilities.

- Parents become fuller members of the community and are less isolated.

- Positive pre-school experiences mean that parents are more likely to choose mainstream primary schools for their children.

- Staff and children benefit from contact with children and adults who have special or additional needs.

- Good practice in the care and education of children with SEN can improve good practice for all the children in the setting.[1]

Case study

A nursery in a segregated school for physically disabled children in the north of England decided to offer places to able-bodied children from the area. Within days, places for both the morning and the afternoon sessions were taken up and the start date for the scheme was fixed for the beginning of the new term. It got off to a flying start and very soon there was a waiting list of children who wanted a place.

Over the next few months, the parents of both the able-bodied and the physically disabled children began to make relationships and started to see each other socially, arranging coffee mornings at each other's houses, or going out for the evening to a pub or restaurant. Because they lived in different parts of the borough, they would not otherwise have met each other. They came to value their friendships and the support they offered each other, whether or not their child had disabilities.

The practitioners in the nursery heard comments such as 'I didn't realise it, but the disabled kids are actually just the same as any others, aren't they?' or 'Now I know Thomas can get on with other kids, I'm going to put his name down for our local school when he's five.'

Some general principles of inclusion

- Inclusion means *celebrating* the child's *achievements* and *abilities.*
- The philosophy of inclusion means that children with SEN will remain, wherever possible, in a mainstream setting for their education.
- Settings must make arrangements to ensure disabled children have their entitlements met.
- Regardless of children's difficulties, they have the right to be helped to fulfil their potential, in a setting that sees them in *a positive light.*
- Inclusion means:
  - evaluating the resources in the setting and making sure that they are accessible to everyone;
  - selecting appropriate books, making them available to everybody and using them regularly;
  - looking at the physical layout of the room in which disabled children spend most of their time, and adapting it if necessary to enable them to access all the resources and equipment;
  - making sure that every member of the group and their contribution to the day's activities are valued and their opinions are heard and respected by everybody else;
  - ensuring that the children in the setting can meet and interact with a wide range of people who will help them to develop an appreciation of the diversity of talents, backgrounds and cultures of their shared society.

Some strategies for including children with special needs

- Use your setting's baseline measurements and/or the Foundation stage profile to check the child's achievement level, and plan the next targets from that point.
- Involve the child's parents and, if appropriate, the child in planning the IEP. (This is explored at relevant points in the appropriate chapters of this book.)
- Observe the child at work and play – what motivates, stimulates and challenges them? Use this information to plan the IEP and teaching strategies.
- Work towards IEP targets in small steps. If the child has difficulty with any of them, reduce them still further; if the child progresses quickly, challenge them by making the steps a little more demanding.
- When the child achieves success, even if it is not the final target, give lots of praise and some form of reward – something that has meaning for the child. Involve the child in their own record-keeping – filling in achievement charts or putting merit stickers in a folder have a magical effect.
- When the child needs support, work together in a small group or, if possible, in a one-to-one situation, whichever is better for the child.
- If the child has communication difficulties, take the time to learn a signing system such as Makaton, which has symbols as well as text – many children with learning difficulties find this system helpful; the other children in the setting quickly pick it up and become enthusiastic users too. Liaise with a speech and language therapist for this.

Practitioners should:

- try to allocate a key worker to the child;

- always speak to the child in a positive way. For example, 'Come and sit with me, Charlie and we'll share this book' works better than 'Sit down and stop doing that, Charlie';

- make sure they face the child when speaking. In this way, the child will get the whole message without losing either its beginning or its end;

- make sure their facial expression is always relaxed and warm;

- attract the child's attention by gently touching their shoulder and saying their name before giving instructions, information etc. But be aware of whether the child will tolerate this and/or where appropriate, bear safety and legal issues/implications in mind;

- give instructions in small, easy-to-digest 'bite size' amounts, if necessary one step at a time;

- keep to the daily routine as much as possible;

- work with the child using games and play-based activities to achieve their targets;

- watch for any personality clashes – change the routine to avoid difficult situations, if necessary. Be aware that child–practitioner clashes can happen as well as child–child problems;

- establish a positive and mutually supportive relationship with the child's parents;

- learn to use equipment, communication systems or other special facilities that the child may have.

The setting's environment

- Reassess the furniture. Does the child need special or adapted furniture or equipment?
- Have adjustable tables, or a selection of different height surfaces.
- Position tables near natural light, or good quality artificial light.
- Make sure that chairs are the right height for a correct posture.
- Use chairs with arms for support and security in a sitting position.
- Make sure there is space between tables and other pieces of furniture to allow ease of moving around the room without collisions.
- Keep furniture and designated areas in the same place.
- Make sure the floor is not polished, to give a more secure foothold and to prevent light reflection.
- Are there any windows at floor level?
- Doors should be opened and closed easily, but not swing back to nip fingers.
- Keep cupboard doors and drawers closed – everyone should do this.
- Have handrails fitted to steps and ramps if necessary. (If you don't need to do this immediately because there aren't any children in the setting who require handrails or ramps, you can include it in your medium-term planning for redecorating and refurbishment of the setting.)
- Are the toilets and hand basins accessible?
- Have a quiet area always available. Make sure it is regarded as a pleasant place where the child can go to 'wind down' – it must never be used as a 'sin bin' or punishment.
- Display pictures, labels and captions etc. at the lowest child's height.
- Keep the layout of apparatus the same.
- Cover sharp and/or extruding corners with foam.
- Keep the floor clear of small items such as pencils, Lego and so on.

Resources, books and equipment

- Put sand and water trays at floor level for easy access by the child who works at floor level. It is also a fun experience for the able-bodied children and, by all playing together, the children are fully included.
- Use big cushions or beanbags to support the child who works and/or plays at floor level.
- Keep easels and stands in good repair – are they steady and secure?
- Can the child hold the paintbrushes, crayons etc.? Use jumbo sizes or wrap standard sized handles in foam rubber.
- Try to exploit all the child's senses in routine activities such as sand or water play. Put colours and/or scents into sand or water.
- Have some musical instruments that vibrate. Have others that don't require vision to play. If you have a wooden floor use it to create vibrations by stamping or thumping on it. Let the children feel the vibrations with their bare feet or their cheeks.
- Have easy-to-find-and-use door and drawer handles – knobs are best.
- Secure small equipment on surfaces using dycem mats (or similar).

- Use persona dolls and books to explore the concept of disability and to develop a positive image of people who have special needs.
- At story time, circle time or group discussions, use dolls with aids such as glasses, callipers or a hearing aid, as part of the session.
- Provide books with clear, bold images and pictures.
- Read books and stories that feature characters with a disability, but not necessarily as the main character.
- Have books and equipment on shelves that are at accessible heights.
- Make labels, cards etc. with tactile materials such as sandpaper, velvet, polystyrene, bubble wrap and so on.
- Have a variety of balls for catching and throwing games – for example, some with a bell inside, others with different surfaces such as smooth rubber or tennis balls, balls of different weights, balls that move erratically, balls with different smells made by soaking tennis balls in different scents.
- Is the small play equipment accessible? Is the outdoor equipment accessible?

You can find a useful framework for developing inclusive practices in *Index for Inclusion: Developing Learning and Participation in Schools*,[2] a publication of the Centre for Studies on Inclusive Education. The *Index* was circulated to all LEAs, primary, secondary and special schools and should be available from your LEA. You will find the contact details for obtaining a copy at the end of this chapter.

Differentiation

Differentiation should now be an automatic part of planning the early years curriculum (of any curriculum in fact) to make sure that children with SEN are not only included, but also achieve success and make progress. In essence, differentiation means that the practitioner should plan activities in steps that are small enough for the child with SEN to achieve the success that leads to learning. Differentiation can mean many things: providing specialised equipment such as adapted scissors, a hearing aid or a chair with supporting arms to those children who need them; using sign language or pictures and symbols if the child relies on these; even something as simple as adjusting the times that a particular activity is offered if the child does it better at another part of the day. You will know best how to adapt and adjust what is on offer and how to offer it according to the child's needs.

Case studies

Jeffrey worked from a wheelchair and was never able to have a turn at being 'milk monitor' because he couldn't take the beakers and biscuits to the other children who sat at their tables. The practitioners changed the system so that the children collected their snack from the monitor who handed it out from a central 'distribution' point before taking it to their places. In this way, Jeffrey was able to be included on the Snack Monitor rota along with all the other children.

Harvinder found working in whole-class sessions extremely stressful and often displayed inappropriate behaviour in that situation. The practitioners decided to work with Harvinder in a one-to-one session beforehand, exploring the planned activity or teaching point so that Harvinder already knew the content of the whole-class session. He would then start the whole-class work with the support of his key worker and as soon as he began to behave inappropriately, he and the key worker would move to the quiet area to complete the activity. Harvinder was eventually able to tolerate whole-class situations for longer periods of time and his inappropriate behaviour decreased.

Emily has partial sight and finds difficulty in seeing line drawings. Her practitioner makes sure that the books available for Emily are illustrated with photographs. Emily also needs a lamp that can be focused on her work, and this is on loan to the setting by the LEA's Visually Impaired Support Service.

Greater emphasis on the involvement of both the child and the parents

The *Code of Practice* recognises that when the child's parents/carers and (where possible and appropriate) the child are involved in the planning and implementation of programmes of work, Play Plans and/or IEPs, the outcome is more likely to be successful and the child has a greater chance of making progress and learning. It always pays dividends when the parents are involved – the children who see home and setting working together will be more committed themselves. Be prepared though for parents who refuse outright to become involved, and for those who promise to do follow-up work at home, but for various reasons they don't manage to do it.

Involving the child

- If it is appropriate to speak to the child about the difficulties they are experiencing, do this in an ethos of 'We're all special in our own way; we're all good at some things; we all need help with some things'.

- Make sure that the child understands the targets of their IEP. If the child can see where they're going and why – like all of us when we have a programme to follow, whether it's a diet or a course of treatment! – they will be happier to be involved and to be motivated.

- Explain to the child that parents, the staff in the early years setting and the child are a team, working together to help them.

- Talk to the child about what it is that makes them need help. For example, they might have difficulty with speaking or hearing or learning things. Explain that people or things are there to help them overcome their difficulties.

- Be sensitive to the potential stress and anxiety that the assessment and subsequent review procedures may cause the child. Anxieties can develop as a result of simply not knowing or not understanding what's going on. Watch for any signs of this and talk calmly and positively to the child about what it's all about.

- Make sure the child understands the role played by outside agents. It might be a bit scary for the child when 'outsiders' become involved – again try to alleviate any anxiety.

- If it is possible, arrange with the people from outside agencies who are involved with your setting to visit occasionally, so the children get used to them. If this can be done at drop-off or collection time so that the parents can establish a relationship with them too, then all the better. This helps to reduce the perception of 'them' being 'brought in' if this becomes necessary at Early Years Action Plus.

- Take the time to find out about advocacy services for children or pupil support services that are available locally. The child's parents (or sometimes the children themselves) might feel isolated or in need of more support. If you give them contact details they can use this later if they want to.

- Allocate a key member of staff to the child. Knowing there is one adult whom the child can go to is an important part of this network of support for the child.

- If the child is already involved with outside agents, explain that you will all be working together to help the child.

- If the child is 'looked after' by the local authority and does not have natural parents to offer support, make sure you establish a positive and cooperative relationship with the carers. It is as crucial for the 'looked after' child to see that foster parents or house parents are involved, as it is for a child from a more traditional background. Let the child know that these adults care for them and are a valued part of the team too.

Involving the parents/carers

- Be sensitive to the parents' feelings, especially if the problems have only recently been identified. The parents are likely to be less stressed if the child's problem was identified at birth, for example Down's Syndrome, since they will have had three or four years to come to terms with the situation. But if the diagnosis has only recently been made, they might be going through a grieving process.

- Be prepared for a variety of reactions. Disbelief, denial, grief, self-blame ('Did I do something wrong during the pregnancy/birth/early days?'), even aggression. There is also 'Thank goodness, someone's believed me and given it a name!' There can be over-protection and extreme anxiety. You need to understand and make allowances for any of these.

- Give the parents time to talk. Be there to listen, but use your time wisely – you and the other children also have needs, so make sure they are met too.

- Always give encouragement and positive feedback to parents about their child's progress. Tell them about the child's achievements, good behaviour and targets they have reached. It is particularly important for parents of early years children to have something positive to hang on to – even something like 'Joe's tried really hard today, Mrs Bloggs and we're really pleased with his efforts.'

- Be truthful – don't tell them that the child has achieved something unless they really have! There's nothing worse for parents than Mrs X saying Walter is doing really well when Mrs Y says he's struggling at the same thing!

- Explain all programmes and strategies that will be used at school or in the setting. Parents are usually keen to know about their child's programme. Always explain to them any changes you want to make, and why – you need their support if the programme is to work.

- Work together with the parents on any programmes suggested by outside agents. The benefits of activities that are reinforced at home are enormous. Always tell parents about any discussions that take place if an outside agent 'pops in' to talk to you and the parents weren't present.

- Without being patronising, always give the parents credit for any support or good work carried out at home. Their sense of isolation will reduce and they will have the knowledge that they are *doing* something for their child and doing it well.

- Be a mutual support group – discovering what motivates a child and sharing that information will have benefits all round. The parents know how their child reacts to things at home; you know how they react in the setting – sharing this information will give you all a resource of knowledge about the child that can be used when planning activities and programmes.

- Find out the contact details of relevant societies, associations, self-help groups etc., and pass them on to the parents. They may not want this information immediately – it depends on the stage they are at after identification of the problem – but they may be eternally grateful for it later, and you may find the information useful too!

- The best source of information about a child's problems is the parents, so ask them everything you want to know. When you know a child is going to be admitted, read about the difficulties or condition, but don't spend an inordinate amount of time on this – at this point, it will be theoretical and probably won't mean very much to you. So wait until the child is paying the introductory visits and ask the parents. Then after the child is admitted and you've got to know them better, do some more background reading. You'll find that you'll be saying 'Yes – that's exactly what Joe's like' or 'Joe does that a bit, but nothing like as much as that' and so on. Even children with the same difficulty or 'condition' will rarely present in the same way, or exactly as described in the literature.

- Plan appropriate activities. So for example, don't give a threading activity to a child who has difficulties with fine motor skills and can't yet manage the beads and thread (unless of course you're following a planned physiotherapy programme with the child). If the activity is not helping the child to achieve their target, then change it. In other words, *Match the Game to the Aim* – this is crucial for success.

- Establish a home/setting system of communication to tell about:
    - the current target that the child is aiming for and its relevance to the particular Early Learning Goal, or Stepping Stone of the Foundation stage or National Curriculum, so the parents can see your longer term aim;
    - which games and activities are being used to achieve the target;
    - how to follow up the learning at home (i.e. how the parents can repeat the game or activity at home, possibly using the same games and activities as in the setting);
    - a record of the number of times the activity was done, how long it took and the outcome (it is important to record what the child *can* do and not what they can't, for example, 'Walter can identify his name card from among five others', not 'Walter still can't say what sound his name begins with');
    - examples of the child's involvement in their own record-keeping. For example, Joe might have his own book of stickers or a chart with balloons to colour in.

- Emphasise to the parents that as soon as the child shows any boredom, distraction or distress, they should stop doing the activity. If the child is forced to continue, they won't enjoy the activity, therefore they won't gain anything from it and they may even turn against it, so defeating your whole aim.

- Keep your money! Often, standard early years equipment is the best resource, and the repertoire of songs, rhymes and finger games are the most valuable – you may not need specialised equipment. This is especially so for developing language skills, literacy skills, memory retention, sequencing, auditory perception and discrimination, and so on. If you do need some specialised equipment, it is possible that you will be able to borrow some for the time that the child is with you. If you buy something, you might never use it again after the child has left you, and you've wasted precious money. So ask the local support services, physiotherapy department, occupational therapy department etc. to see what you can have on loan.

- If the parents are not familiar with the songs, rhymes and games used in the setting, invite them to sit in on a few sessions at drop-off or collection time. They will very quickly pick up the technique. This also has a spin-off in that you begin to develop a closer relationship with the parents as they become more involved in your setting and its daily routine.

One idea to involve the parents is to develop Play Plans with them for use at home. See page 42 for a Play Plan form, page 43 for an example of a completed Play Plan, and Part 3 for more discussion of Play Plans.

New rights of appeal for parents

LEAs have a duty to set up a system of preventing and dealing with disagreements that may arise between the authority and the parents of a child with SEN, or between the school and the parents. The LEA has to appoint independent people for this to ensure that disagreements are handled in a neutral and fair way, and the authority must inform the child's parents of their rights to use this service. A disagreement could arise if, for example, the parents are not satisfied with some aspects of the school's provision for their child, or if at the stage of Statutory Assessment they feel that some element in the Statement of Special Educational Needs is unfair or incorrect, or even that they wish to challenge the LEA's decision *not* to make a Statutory Assessment.

If the parents feel that the disagreement is not being resolved to their satisfaction, they have the right to appeal to the SEN Tribunal. This can be stressful and time-consuming and it is in everybody's interests to resolve disagreements where possible, without recourse to the SEN Tribunal. But the facility is there if parents feel strongly that they want to pursue their case.

Special Educational Needs Coordinator – SENCO

The early years setting must establish the role of Special Educational Needs Coordinator (SENCO) and allocate the post to one of the practitioners. The role of the SENCO at each stage of the *Code* is discussed in the appropriate chapters of this book.

Special Educational Needs Policy

The revised *Code of Practice* requires early years settings to write an SEN policy, and to publish it for parents or any other interested parties. The policy should be planned and written with the concept of inclusion at its core, and should be constantly monitored and reviewed. It is a working document and as such should be changed and adapted, as the needs and practices of the setting change and adapt.

- The *management* of the SEN policy is the manager/head's responsibility.
- The *planning, writing* and *publishing* of it should be done by everybody appropriately involved with the setting.
- The day-to-day *operation* of the SEN policy is the SENCO's responsibility.
- The actual *implementation* of the policy is the responsibility of all other members of staff within their own area.

The setting's SEN policy must provide:

1. *Information about the setting's provisions* including:

   - *The objectives of the SEN policy* (i.e. ask yourself 'What are our aims in our SEN provision?' 'Are we aiming for inclusion?' Think about this in real terms – the actual 'hands-on' logistics of putting the policy into practice – rather than wonderful theory or philosophy that sounds good but isn't true inclusion).
   - *The name of the SENCO* (make sure everyone involved in the setting knows who this is; post it up and change the position of the notice every few weeks to avoid 'familiarity blindness').
   - *The arrangements for coordinating provision for children with SEN* (i.e. ask yourselves, 'How do we intend to cater for children with SEN in terms of resources, staffing, time

etc.?' This is where the reality begins to kick in. You have to look at the way your setting is organised, run, staffed and equipped, looking at each of these and saying 'Does each element include *all* our children?').

- *The setting's admission arrangements for children with SEN* (i.e. ask yourselves things like, 'How will we approach the way that children with SEN are admitted?', 'Will we have a transition/familiarisation period?', 'Will we invite parents to stay with the child initially?' etc. Are you flexible enough to adapt these arrangements if necessary? For example, suppose you set up a system where the children spend an hour per morning initially, gradually building up over three weeks to a full session; then you realise that little Walter just can't cope with the full session yet – can you adjust so that his admission is paced to meet his needs?).

- *The SEN specialisms that the setting may have to offer* (for example, staff with a specialist qualification or access to a specialist facility. As the practitioners' training opportunities are taken up, your setting will be building up a resource of knowledge and expertise that will be invaluable, so let everybody know about it!).

2. *Information about the setting's policies for identifying, assessing and providing* for children with SEN including:

- *The allocation of resources* (so when you are planning your resources and how to use them, ask yourselves 'What?' – have we got equipment, games, activities etc. that can be used by *all* children?; 'How much?' – is there only one chunky paintbrush when we could really do with half a dozen?; 'When?' – do we use the cooking equipment on Friday mornings only? What a pity, because Fred attends in the afternoons; 'Where?' – do we always have the water play in the water tray and stand? What a pity when Lucy can't access it because she works at floor level; and 'Who?' – could the volunteer who takes some of the children for sewing squeeze in another body who'd really benefit from the experience?).

- *The arrangements for identifying and assessing special educational needs* (i.e. ask yourselves, 'Who will do it? When? Where? How?' For example, will it be done by the child's own practitioner, the SENCO, the setting head/manager? Will it be done at a set time, or a time when the assessor happens to be 'free' to do it? Will it be done in the setting's normal daily activity sessions or a special assessment/observation session? What form will the assessments take? For example, will you use the Foundation stage profile, standardised assessments, observations [and what type of observation?] and so on?).

- *The procedures for reviewing a child's special educational needs* (i.e. when, where and how will reviews be carried out? Who will be involved? Some of the guidance in the *Code of Practice* gives you suggestions about these arrangements, but some only you can sort out. For example, the where and how – you know your setting's facilities, timetable, staffing, clientele and so on, and with these factors involved in the decision-making, your arrangements will be unique to you).

- *The arrangements for providing access to a balanced and broadly based curriculum* (i.e. whether the child is following the Foundation stage curriculum or the National Curriculum – how will you make sure all children *regardless of their ability* have the opportunities and experiences of the full early years curriculum? This may mean adjusting the timetable, the venue, the staffing, the resources and equipment and so on, to open up to the children with SEN everything that's on offer to the rest of the group).

- *The arrangements for inclusion in the setting as a whole* (this should be the main consideration behind the policy. How will you make sure you efficiently implement inclusion? It is the core of the concept and everything you plan needs to come back to this central premise).

- *The criteria for evaluating the success of the SEN policy* (i.e. when and how will you review the policy? How will you decide its strengths and weaknesses? How will you make any required changes? As you use the policy and live with it from day to day, the little wrinkles inherent in it will become apparent – only you will know how serious or otherwise the weaknesses are and how quickly you need to address them. There isn't a blueprint or perfect policy, because each setting is individual).

- *The arrangements for dealing with complaints about the SEN provision* (i.e. what procedures will you put in place to make sure that complaints are dealt with fairly and efficiently? A substantial part of the *Code* deals with the new rights of appeal and tribunal procedures that are in place for parents to invoke. But ideally you don't want problems to get that far – have in place an 'in-house' procedure that can address problems in an amicable way between yourselves and to the satisfaction of the parents).

3. *Information about the setting's staffing policies and partnership with other establishments* including:

- *The arrangements for staff training in the area of special educational needs* (i.e. how will you make sure staff can access information and professional training? Your Early Years Development & Childcare Partnership [EYDCP] [NB: at the time of writing the phasing out of EYDCPs was under discussion] and local education authority [LEA] will have this on offer either in terms of in-house training, or information and advice about accessing training offered by other providers. The onus is on the setting to make sure you can tap this source when you need to).

- *The use made of outside agencies and support services* (i.e. How often? Where? When? Do you have a procedure for involving the parents in inter-agency discussions?).

- *The arrangements for partnership with parents* (this includes access to Parent Partnership Services and/or Independent Parental Support. Do you have procedures for making sure parents are made aware of their rights? Do you have arrangements in place for parents who do not speak English? Or those who have alternative communication systems themselves, for example sign language?).

- *The links with other establishments* (for example, schools, childminding networks and other early years settings. Who, with, and how are the links maintained?).

- *The links with other outside agencies* (for example, social services, health, education welfare services and voluntary organisations. How are links with these maintained?).

During your policy planning sessions ask yourselves the following questions:
- Why do we need it?
- Who is it for?
- What needs to be in it?
- When will it be used?
- How should it be worded?
- Where do we start?[3]

and continually bear in mind that the policy should be:
- relevant;
- owned;
- practised;
- reviewed.[4]

For an example of an early years SEN policy document, see the Appendix on page 75.

Individual Education Plans (IEPs) to focus only on what is additional to and different from the rest of the curriculum

Since the needs of many children can be met through the routine differentiation of the curriculum, at this stage practitioners do not have to plan, write and implement IEPs as such. For example, you might know that Soozie needs a little more time than the others to assimilate a concept and a few more practice sessions to consolidate the skills involved, so you make sure she gets the opportunities she needs. In this situation, you will have differentiated for her, but you would not need to write a specific IEP, although you would make a note of the differentiation in Soozie's records.

It is important to keep careful records of any differentiation that you do, since a child may eventually need to have an IEP after all. 'Evidence' provided by earlier differentiated work could prove to be very useful for planning the IEP and may even be helpful if the child moves through the later levels of the *Code of Practice*.

IEPs need to be used when the child continues to cause concern due to a lack of progress despite a carefully differentiated curriculum. They should then be used as a record of what is being done for and with the child that is different from the rest of the curriculum and/or in addition to it.

There is further discussion about the planning, writing and implementation of IEPs in Part 3 of this book.

Conclusion

The main points explored in this chapter on the revised *SEN Code of Practice* are that:

- there are three stages of intervention;
- children in *all* early years provision are now included in the legislation;
- a greater emphasis is placed on the involvement of both the child and the parents in decision making and planning;
- there is a new right of appeal for parents;
- the Individual Education Plans (IEPs) should focus only on what is *additional to* and *different from* the rest of the curriculum.

References

1. *All Together: How to Create Inclusive Services for Disabled Children and their Families. A Practical Handbook for Early Years Workers*, M. Dickins and J. Denziloe, National Children's Bureau, 2nd edition, 2003.
2. *Index for Inclusion: Developing Learning and Participation in Schools*, T. Booth, M. Ainscow, K. Black-Hawkins, M. Vaughan and L. Shaw (Centre for Studies on Inclusive Education), available from the Centre for Studies on Inclusive Education, Room 2S203, 5 Block, Frenchay Campus, Coldharbour Lane, Bristol, BS16 1QU. Telephone 01173 444 007.
3. 'Policies and Procedures', *Practical Pre-school*, Liz Wilcock, July 2001.
4. 'Policies and Procedures', *Practical Pre-school*, Liz Wilcock, July 2001.

PART 2

Expressing concern

Early years practitioners are experts in spotting when a child seems to be experiencing difficulties. Depending on the nature of the difficulty, you may be able to identify the problem almost immediately or you may have a general concern about the child without being able to pinpoint something specific.

The *SEN Code of Practice* highlights the importance of making sure that children should build on their previous experiences to develop skills in the six areas of learning outlined in the Foundation stage curriculum: personal, social and emotional development; communication, language and literacy; mathematical development; knowledge and understanding of the world; physical development; and creative development.

If you have a concern about a child, you should first of all share your concerns with the child's parents or carers and find out how they view the situation. You should monitor the child and keep careful records of what you find, using these to decide whether the child is or is not making adequate progress within your setting.

According to the *Code of Practice*, adequate progress can be defined in a number of ways. For example, the child can be said to make adequate progress if *the gap closes* between their achievements and those of their peer group, or is *prevented from becoming wider*; the child makes adequate progress if their performance is *similar to that of their peer group* when measured by the same attainment baseline assessments, but less than that of the majority of their peer group; if the child *matches or betters their own rate of progress* or has achievement levels that *ensure access to the full early years curriculum*, they have made adequate progress; if the child shows to have *improved in self-help, social or personal skills*, or have *improved in their behaviour*, they are deemed to have made adequate progress.

If it becomes apparent that a child is not making adequate progress in any or all of the areas of learning in the Foundation stage curriculum, you should:

- speak to the child's parents about your concerns and ask them if they have any information that might have a bearing on the difficulties being experienced by the child;
- observe the child and do relevant assessments, including the setting's own assessment procedures and/or the Foundation stage profile;
- complete a form expressing your concerns (see below);
- differentiate the child's curriculum appropriately;
- monitor the child closely;
- keep careful records of the child's progress;
- speak to the SENCO (with the parents' permission) on a 'need to know' basis;
- review whether and when the child should move forward to Early Years Action.

Observing the child

Observations are a fundamental part of early years practice and their value cannot be overstated. Because they provide a record of what the child can do, they should be used in a variety of situations such as play, self-chosen activities, structured activities and adult-led activities. In this way, the practitioner can build up a picture of the child's achievements and abilities across the full spectrum of what is on offer. But making the observations is only the first stage, the information-gathering exercise. After that, the practitioner must use the information gathered to make an assessment of the child's overall achievement level, and to plan towards the next level that the child is going to aim for.

Observations are also useful for sharing information about the child with both the parents and other professionals. You can use the information to discuss the child with the parents, who will be able to see how their child functions in the setting; and you can share the information with other professionals, particularly those who have only just met the child, to help them gain a fuller insight into the child's abilities.

There are two basic types of observation: the Continuous (or Narrative) observation and the Focused (or Targeted) observation.

Continuous (or Narrative) observations

These are usually carried out by all practitioners in the setting. They consist of short notes jotted down at any time on a day-to-day basis, forming a record of the child's daily progress and any specific achievements. They help build up a longer-term picture of the child's development. They record briefly what the child does, together with short related assessment statements, linking in with the relevant targets of the child's curriculum and/or the Individual Education Plan. They are dated and initialled by the practitioner(s) and put into the child's profile folder.

Focused (or Targeted) observations

These are usually carried out by one practitioner, less frequently and with a more specific aim in mind. The observation takes place across a fixed time, usually 10 or 15 minutes, where the practitioner records what the child does and says. They are usually carried out at a time agreed between the practitioners in the setting, to enable the observer to be released from contact, leading activities or teaching. According to the child's needs, the number of focused observations per week, half-term or term should be agreed by all the staff involved with the child. Observation records are dated and signed by the observer.

While observing, the practitioner can leave out anything the child does that bears no relation to the observation focus. So, for example, there is no need to write 'Walter went for a tissue and blew his nose' if the focus of the observation is to assess Walter's early maths skills.

Because of the 'busyness' of the setting, the practitioner may choose to make notes with key words and write the observation up properly, either immediately or as soon as possible afterwards.

The observation should be objective and factual to ensure its accuracy, since the practitioner's memory can play tricks when overtaken by other events in the setting.

To be objective and factual, the record must state only what happened, not the observer's opinion of what happened. For example, 'Walter tore up Katie's picture and then hit her' is more objective and factual than 'Walter behaved badly towards Katie'. The first statement shows exactly what Walter did; the second shows nothing beyond the observer's disapproval of what happened. 'Behaved badly' is a subjective phrase, meaning different things to different people; it does not tell the reader anything relevant about the incident.

Practitioners will usually do focused observations (as opposed to continuous observations) when they need to collect information about a child who is causing concern, and where specific evidence of that child's difficulties is needed. It is very important to repeat an observation if it seems to highlight any difficulties that the child is experiencing. One observation will not give enough evidence of a difficulty, and so the child must be observed at least once again, preferably a couple more times. It is also a good idea to ask another practitioner to conduct an observation, to discover whether they identify the same concerns.

While conducting an observation, it is important that the practitioner is a 'fly-on-the-wall', as this is how subjective information will be gleaned. Even if the child does something that requires adult intervention, the observer must resist the temptation to become involved, leaving it to the other practitioners to sort out the situation, while continuing to make notes on what is happening.

The information gleaned from the observations can then be used to plan specific targets, strategies and methods for enabling the child to make progress.

You will find examples of completed observations on pages 25 and 27, and blank photocopiable observation forms on pages 24 and 26.

Forms for expressing concerns

Settings may already have in place a form for expressing concerns, either from the LEA or their own self-designed format. An example of a photocopiable Expression of Concern Form can be found on page 28. It can be used as it stands or adapted to suit each setting's own particular situation. The form records the most important pieces of information, so settings designing their own forms should make sure that these sections are all included in the final version. When you complete the form, you should share this with the child's parents and make sure they are happy with what you have written. Some parents may feel anxious or threatened by the situation and you should be very careful not to create any stress for them. Avoid the use of terminology such as 'registration' or 'official', which may have negative associations for some parents. This may be the beginning of a longer collaboration between you and the parents, and it is important from the outset that you gain their trust and confidence.

You will find an example of a completed Expression of Concern Form on page 29.

Differentiating the curriculum

Differentiation was briefly discussed in Part 1. When a child seems to find more difficulty in learning than the others in their group, the practitioner should make adjustments for this and adapt the activities, presentation, teaching styles, timing and so on, to make sure the child can achieve the skill or concept being aimed for.

You can do this by looking at the final target and breaking it down into small steps that are done one at a time and thoroughly consolidated before moving on to the next one. This way the child will achieve the target through a graduated approach that allows for their personal learning style and level. Record your plan using a form such as the photocopiable Small Steps Planning Form, on page 30.

Case study

Soozie Bubble has difficulty in dressing and undressing herself, particularly with buttons and buttonholes. Soozie becomes very upset when she changes for PE sessions and when she uses the toilet, because she has such a struggle with her clothes. Soozie's Mum always dresses her in dungarees with button fastenings and these create the biggest problems for Soozie. Also Soozie can't yet tie laces but, as she wears shoes with Velcro fastenings, this is not an immediate problem. Soozie has commented several times that the other children 'are good at buttons but me can't do them'.

Soozie's Small Steps Planning Form which was completed by Soozie's Early Years key worker is on page 31.

Definition of Special Educational Needs

The *Code of Practice* says that 'children have special educational needs if they have a *learning difficulty* which calls for *special educational provision* to be made for them'.[1]

Some children can have a learning difficulty in its own right, but others may have learning difficulties that arise from or exist alongside other problems. According to the *Code of Practice* children have a learning difficulty if they are experiencing greater difficulties in learning than the majority of children in their peer group. They also have learning difficulties if they have a disability which prevents them from attending a local school which offers the education and facilities generally available to all the children in their peer group living in their LEA. A third definition is given, for children who are below school age and who come under one or both of the first two definitions (or would do if SEN provision was not made for them).

The *Code of Practice* outlines categories of the difficulties a child may be experiencing, but it does recognise that these difficulties may fall into several of the categories outlined. While acknowledging that there is a wide range of special educational needs, the *Code* addresses a number of broad areas of need, including:

- *Communication and interaction*, such as speech and language delay and/or disorders, specific learning difficulties, or partial hearing/deafness.
  So, for example, a child who has dyslexia or speech dyspraxia may be included here; or a child with hearing difficulties which could range from 'glue ear' to profound deafness; or the full range of disorders on the autistic spectrum, including Asperger's Syndrome and semantic-pragmatic disorders.

- *Cognition and learning*, such as moderate, severe or profound learning difficulties, specific learning difficulties, physical and/or sensory problems or autistic spectrum disorders.
  Already there is an apparent overlap here, with difficulties like dyslexia or dyspraxia, or autistic spectrum disorders being included in this category, as well as that of communication and interaction. Children who require a specific programme to help the development of their cognitive skills, such as the Portage scheme, would also come into this group of difficulties.

- *Behavioural, emotional and social development*, such as challenging or inappropriate behaviour, withdrawn and/or isolated behaviour or hyperactivity.
  The hyperactive child may well be the little person who has been diagnosed as having Attention Deficit Disorder or Attention Deficit/Hyperactive Disorder (ADD or AD/HD). Also included would be the child who has immature social skills, and the child who has challenging or inappropriate behaviour because of other complex special needs. Watch out for the quiet child who is very easy to overlook in the hubbub of an early years setting because they are not drawing attention to themselves.

- *Sensory and/or physical*, such as partial sight/blindness, partial hearing/deafness, whether temporary or permanent; and motor problems.
  As already mentioned, the range of hearing disabilities can be from intermittent hearing loss due to 'glue ear' right through to profound deafness. On the vision side, the range can be from operable cataracts, for example, to a total lack of vision.
  Motor difficulties can arise as a result of conditions such as dyspraxia or cerebral palsy, or they could be caused by trauma such as head and/or limb injuries sustained in an accident.

- *Medical conditions*
  The commonest medical conditions early years practitioners are likely to come across in early years settings are asthma, eczema, diabetes and allergies of either foods or substances such as plastics or even sunlight. You might also encounter children with cerebral palsy, epilepsy, haemophilia, HIV or cystic fibrosis. There is no need to worry about working with a child with a medical condition as there is lots of support and advice from the good network of agencies that you will become part of.

A medical condition does not necessarily mean a child has SEN. This is an important point to remember – it is easy to become blinded by the condition and assume that it affects the child's *educational* abilities.

'It is the child's educational needs rather than a medical diagnosis that must be considered.'[2]

A condition not properly managed could hinder access to education. For this reason, if you are unsure about the best way of managing a child's condition in the setting, then ask for help and advice from the child's parents and the medical professionals who are involved with the child.

There may be a direct impact on the child through a condition affecting cognitive or physical abilities or behavioural or emotional state. So, for example, a child with spina bifida may have learning difficulties, or a child with cerebral palsy may have physical and motor problems, or a child with autism may have quite profound emotional difficulties.

There may be an indirect impact through the child's education being disrupted because of treatment or psychological effects on child and/or the family. It may be, for example, that a child with cancer who is undergoing radiotherapy or chemotherapy may sometimes be too sick to attend the setting; the family may sometimes go through periods of depression because of a poor prognosis, and so on.

An example of psychological effects might be trauma caused by a sudden and tragic bereavement. All of this will affect the child and their performance.

The effects of a medical condition can be intermittent. You need to be aware of this since the child's performance and/or progress may appear to be erratic, but the condition could be the cause.

How are the child's difficulties identified?

The field of SEN is so vast, and each child is unique, but there are some signs that the early years practitioner can watch for, which might indicate that a child is having difficulties and may also have special educational needs.

General learning difficulties

Be aware of the child who:

- scores poorly on assessments or profiles in comparison with the other children of the same age in their group;
- has levels of development (in all or specific areas) and play which are markedly lower than those of the other children;
- has difficulty in acquiring skills, particularly in communication and interaction, literacy and numeracy;
- has difficulty in dealing with abstract ideas and/or generalising concepts from personal experience;
- makes little or no progress despite involvement in the nursery curriculum and fails to achieve the targets set;
- makes little or no progress despite involvement in a differentiated curriculum.

Developmental delay can be included as a general learning difficulty since, whatever its cause, it can prevent the child from making progress. It is probably something that an early years practitioner is likely to identify very quickly and with confidence, since the developmental milestones will be very familiar. A developmental delay may be the result of other primary difficulties or special needs, but sometimes it is the result of poor stimulation or lack of opportunities for the child to explore the world around them.

Often, the child's developmental progress can be kick-started simply by their involvement in a rich early years environment and curriculum, and the child can catch up with the peer group very quickly. If this is not so in spite of a differentiated programme for the child, you may need to speak to the parents, asking permission to approach the appropriate agents for help and advice.

Physical, motor or sensory disabilities

Watch the child's physical and motor skills and notice if they:

- have difficulty in coordinating their hands and feet;
- experience problems in balancing;
- have poor gross and/or fine motor skills;
- move around clumsily.

The child may have visual difficulties if they:

- hold books and objects close to their face to look at them;
- always sit at the front for stories or television and then strain to look at the book or TV;
- bang into or trip over objects;
- have a lack of confidence when moving around the room and/or show anxiety about banging into things;
- find difficulty in focusing on an object or have problems in eye-tracking
- have difficulty in doing activities that require visual skills and/or have difficulty with hand–eye coordination;
- have unusual eye movements such as roving or 'trembling' of the eyeball;
- display abnormal social interaction or autistic type behaviours;
- hold their head in an unusual position;
- display eye-poking, rocking or other 'blindisms'.

The children may have hearing difficulties if they:

- concentrate intensively on the faces and body gestures of the adults in the setting;
- either do not follow instructions, follow instructions only sometimes and/or follow instructions wrongly;
- do not respond to their name, especially if you call them from behind;
- watch the other children before doing an action, and then copy the others;
- appear to need more visual input and support during activities than the other children in the group;
- behave inappropriately or seem to be frustrated without any apparent cause;
- do not react to loud or unexpected noises;
- shout or talk too loudly without realising they are doing so;
- have delayed speech or speech that is difficult to understand;
- change their voice tone while they are speaking;
- have difficulty doing activities that require listening skills;
- have discharges from their ear(s), which do not seem to clear up or which occur quite frequently;
- tilt their head when listening to stories, instructions and so on;
- appear to be in a world of their own or showing autistic type behaviours.

If you suspect that the child has a sensory problem, it is extremely important to speak to their parents. Ask whether the child's eyes have been tested recently, if you think there is a problem with their vision, or whether their hearing has been checked if you think the difficulty stems from that. A simple initial investigation might pick up a difficulty at this stage that could cause more problems if left to get worse. It may be that there isn't a problem; it may be that for a while the child needs glasses or a grommet, until the situation improves; it may be that something more complex needs to be investigated and the appropriate help given to the child.

Whatever the outcome, it is better to ask for the child to be checked and find there isn't anything amiss after all, than to leave it and let the child continue failing for the want of the correct support.

Medical conditions

A child who has a medical condition may well enter the early years setting with the condition already diagnosed. If they have to come in each morning with an inhaler, oil-based cream, insulin and so on, you need to check the setting's and/or local education authority's policy on medicine in settings and schools. If you are likely to be involved in administering treatment, you need to have advice and guidance in this from the child's parents, the health visitor and/or the child's GP.

For private and non-maintained settings, the same precautions apply. You would also be wise to adopt the following policies before agreeing to administer or supervise the administration of medicines:

- Make sure you have written authorisation from the child's parents.
- Check that the establishment's insurance policy covers the administration of medication.
- Administer medicines in the presence of another member of staff. There are two reasons for this – so that the administration of the medication is witnessed and monitored by a second party, and so that in the absence of one of the members of staff, the other can take over.

Emotional and behavioural difficulties

Emotional and behavioural problems sometimes become clear very quickly after admission to the setting. Look out for the child who:

- is verbally and/or physically aggressive with other children and/or adults;
- is introverted or withdrawn;
- is troubled or worried;
- is loud and inappropriately outgoing;
- behaves in a way which is inappropriate for their chronological age;
- behaves in a way which appears strange or socially inappropriate;
- behaves in a way that may cause self-injury;
- has difficulty in remaining on task, despite support and encouragement from an adult;
- disrupts the setting's routine on a fairly regular basis;
- fails to make the progress expected of them;
- is absent frequently or has periods on non-attendance;
- has spurts of uncooperative behaviour;
- has unpredictable behaviour and/or erratic attitudes to learning;
- appears to be uninterested in the activities and games on offer;
- seems to be over-dependent on adults;
- seems to be hyperactive.

Sometimes, however, a child can have a temporary behavioural difficulty because of something happening at home. For example, a grandparent or a well-loved pet may have died, a new baby may have been born, Dad may have gone to prison, parents may have split up and so on. All these factors will affect a child and, as time passes and the home situation settles, the child's difficulties may fade away. Speak sensitively to the child's parents to find out whether anything at home could be the cause of the difficulties.

Never question a child about their home circumstances – always ask the adults concerned for any information that you want. If, however, the child volunteers information on their own, you can be an important support to the child. Be aware also, however, of potential situations at home that need to be investigated. If, for example, a child discloses something that hints at sexual, physical or emotional abuse, immediately inform the person in the setting who is responsible for child protection issues. Do not question the child in a way that could affect further action – avoid specific questions such as 'Did —— touch you there?' Overzealous and untrained questioning techniques could jeopardise any possible legal action. If there is a problem that needs to be investigated, trained professionals will question the child correctly and appropriately.

It is important to watch how long the child's problems go on for. If they do not seem to be temporary, it is important you keep a record of the episodes of inappropriate behaviour. Often a pattern begins to appear which may show that the episodes of inappropriate behaviour occur at a particular time, in a particular place and/or with a particular person. For example, Walter may start being disruptive round about half past eleven every day, when he is supposed to be doing his IEP session, with Mrs Thingy in the small room where the spare equipment and resources are stored – perhaps he came to school without breakfast and by late morning he is so hungry that he cannot concentrate and he starts to play up; maybe he once saw a huge spider in that room and had a nasty fright, so is now terrified of being in there; or maybe he just dislikes working with Mrs Thingy because there's a simple clash of personalities.

If a pattern does appear, try to identify whatever seems to be the trigger and eliminate it – change the times when he is expected to concentrate hard, so do his IEP first thing in the morning, after you've given him some milk and a biscuit; change the place where he is asked to do his work and let him sit in the Book Corner or at his home-table; or ask another member of staff to do his one-to-one sessions so that he and Mrs Thingy won't have the opportunity to rub each other up the wrong way.

Social difficulties
See whether the child:

- cannot play with other children, or play with them 'normally';
- cannot share or take turns with toys and equipment;
- shows poor or no conversational skills.

These difficulties may be as a result of, among other things, a lack of interaction experience, poor stimulation as a baby or toddler, poor parenting skills or a communication difficulty. If the child's difficulties seem to stem from the home situation, a positive relationship with the parents will go a long way to helping and supporting the child. They will be more likely to take on board any suggestions you might make, in a diplomatic way, for doing things with the child at home. If you think that going to Positive Parenting sessions would help, you will be in a good position to suggest this without causing offence.

Communication difficulties

Look out for the child who:

- hardly ever talks or does not talk at all;
- stammers or has slow speech, but understands what is said to them and what they actually say makes sense;
- has delayed or distorted speech that is difficult to understand;
- has normal speech but what they actually say may be odd or inappropriate in the circumstances;
- has normal speech but seems to have difficulty understanding what is said to them and/or does not respond appropriately to other people;
- speaks at inappropriate times or makes inappropriate remarks;
- laughs very loudly or for too long;
- has difficulty in taking turns during conversations and/or has poor conversational skills;
- has ritualistic or obsessive behaviours or habits;
- has problems communicating through speech and/or other forms of language;
- cannot interact with others with appropriate verbal and/or non-verbal language;
- finds difficulty in reacting normally in social situations or avoids social situations;
- behaves passively and has little or no initiative or curiosity;
- appears to be unaware of other people and their needs or emotions;
- has unusual voice tone, uses bizarre language and/or ritualistic phrases such as advertisement jingles or slogans.

Record-keeping is very important when you suspect a communication difficulty. Even anecdotal evidence can be useful because specific examples of bizarre speech and/or behaviour can often give important clues as to the type of language difficulty the child has. For example, 'cocktail party' conversation can mislead a busy practitioner into thinking the child does not have a language problem, especially if their speech is clear and their grammar is perfect. But if the same social phrases are repeated on a daily basis, without any deeper or relevant conversation coming from the child, you need to be alerted.

In the same way, if the child uses only jingles, such as advertisement slogans, or repetitive phrases regardless of the situation, they need to be checked.

It is crucial to assess the child's receptive and expressive language. They may have sound receptive language but have problems with their speech and/or expressive language; or their expressive language and/or speech may be perfect, even in advance of their chronological age, but their receptive language may be seriously impaired, although this is unusual.

Case study

Jimmy, aged four, began nursery school having been excluded from his local playgroup the previous year, and had no further pre-school experience. Staff noticed his play was either solitary or parallel, and that he always chose to do jigsaws, which he completed while humming tunelessly. When invited to do other activities by the practitioners, he would join in, but rarely took part in a conversation. He would become excited and animated when it was television time.

Eventually, the staff noticed that Jimmy's language was based almost entirely on slogans and jingles from television adverts, and he would use these at various times of the day, but in an appropriate way. For example, when told to put on his coat and hat to go out to play, Jimmy would say, 'C&A Modes, where fashion makes sense'; when the children were discussing their pets and somebody mentioned a dog, Jimmy called out, 'PAL meat for dogs – Prolongs Active Life'; and when one of the children was asked what they ate for breakfast, Jimmy was heard to say to himself, 'Ricicles are twicicles as nicicles'.

In time, Jimmy was diagnosed as having Asperger's Syndrome. The staff in the setting used his interest in advert jingles to encourage early literacy skills and social development.

Specific learning difficulties

It is unlikely that early years practitioners will come across a child who has been identified as having specific learning difficulties, which include specific reading difficulties (dyslexia) and specific numeracy difficulties (dyscalculia). Before these difficulties are spotted, it is probable that the child will be well into the formal literacy and/or numeracy teaching. But it is useful to look out for difficulties with:

- fine or gross motor skills;
- visual or auditory perception if the child does not have any sensory problems. For example, if they are unable to interpret shapes, letters or pictures correctly, or have difficulty in perceiving sounds or phonemes, despite having sound vision and hearing;
- rote learning (nursery rhymes);
- rhythm games or pattern activities;
- short-term memory;
- sequencing and/or organisational skills;
- verbal interaction and/or following instructions;
- hand–eye coordination.

Also look out for:

- higher achievement in areas of learning that do not make demands on the child's weakest skills. For example, the child may have an IEP with targets for some early numeracy concepts and yet may be able to work skilfully on other more advanced areas of maths;
- signs of frustration and/or low self-esteem.

There is no blueprint to identifying and managing special educational needs in early years settings since the range and degree of special needs are so wide. Every case or condition is as unique as the child who has the difficulties. The *Code of Practice* offers a standardised framework of working with the children who have special educational needs, but planning their curriculum, writing their IEPs and helping them to achieve regardless of their specific problems are totally individual matters.

Conclusion

The main points explored in this chapter on expressing concern are that:

- you should try to identify as early as possible any difficulties a child may be experiencing and then speak to the child's parents about your concerns;
- observe the child and do relevant assessments;
- complete a form expressing your concerns;
- differentiate the child's curriculum appropriately;
- monitor the child closely and keep careful records of the child's progress;
- speak to the SENCO (with the parents' permission);
- review whether and when the child should move forward to Early Years Action.

References

1. *Special Educational Needs Code of Practice*, DfES, 2001, 1:3.
2. *Special Educational Needs Code of Practice*, DfES, 2001, 7:64.

Continuous Observation Form

Child's name _____

Date of birth _____

Date	Observation	Area of learning	Planning	Initials

Continuous Observation Form

Child's name ___Joseph Bloggs___

Date of birth ___18.4.00___

Date	Observation	Area of learning	Planning	Initials
4.6.03	Joseph made a chain with thread and beads	PSD	More activities for fine motor skills	JS
4.6.03	Joe recognised his name card from the whole pile	L & L	Find name in other contexts	BM
5.6.03	Joe ripped Melanie's picture	PSD	Plan positive behaviour programme	BM

Focused Observation Form

Child's name _____ Date of birth _____

Date and time of observation _____

Observer_____

Area of learning _____

Learning targets:

1.

2.

3.

Strategies:

1.

2.

3.

Child's name _Joseph Bloggs (3 yrs 2 mnths)_   Date of birth _18.4.00_

Date and time of observation _14 June 2003; 9.30–9.45_

Observer _Jill Smith_

Joe alone at sand tray, pours sand from jug into tub; talking to himself (not clear). Joe goes to sink and fills jug with water, returns to sand tray and pours water into sand at one end. Uses spade to fill tub with sand and make a castle: 'Make a big castle'. Has difficulty getting tub off – sand too wet and castle collapses. Joe frustrated: 'It's all broken'; bangs the pile of wet sand with clenched fist. Moves over to painting area; (no easel free); stands beside Melanie, watches her paint. 'Can I come there?' Melanie refuses. Tries to take the brush from Melanie, slight struggle. Scratches Melanie's hand (deliberate). Melanie cries and goes to BB; Joe takes her place. Pulls Melanie's paper off easel and throws it on floor, looks for fresh paper. Tries to pin new sheet up but fails; starts to paint the easel. BB intervenes, asks why he scratched Melanie. Joe denies it; BB tells him to stop painting the easel. Joe throws brush onto floor and moves to book area.

Area of learning _Personal and social development_

Learning targets:

1. Waiting to take turn if activities not yet available.

2. Being gentle, i.e. controlling urge to scratch, hit etc.

3.

Strategies:

1. Agree system with Joe for rewards for each time he waits to take his turn.

2. Plan programme with rewards for specific time-spans spent with positive behaviour.

3.

Expression of Concern Form

Name of setting _____ Child's name _____

Date of birth _____ Date of admission _____

Area of concern _____

Areas of learning affected (tick boxes as appropriate):

☐ Personal, social and emotional development

☐ Physical development

☐ Communication, language and literacy

☐ Creative development

☐ Mathematical development

☐ Knowledge and understanding of the world

Date(s) of observation(s) _____

Type of observation _____

Findings of observations(s):

Date(s) of assessment(s) _____

Assessment(s) used _____

Findings of assessment(s):

Action taken:

Have the parents been consulted? Yes/No   Parent's signature _____

Has the SENCO been consulted? Yes/No

Signed _____ Position _____

Date _____ Date review due _____

Expression of Concern Form

Name of setting _Fairfield Nursery_   Child's name _Joseph Bloggs_

Date of birth _18 April 2000_   Date of admission _12.2.03_

Area of concern _Inappropriate/challenging behaviour_

Areas of learning affected (tick boxes as appropriate):

☑ Personal, social and emotional development

☐ Physical development

☐ Communication, language and literacy

☐ Creative development

☐ Mathematical development

☐ Knowledge and understanding of the world

Date(s) of observation(s) _13/15/17 Feb 03_

Type of observation _Focused (15 mins)_

Findings of observations(s):

Joe's inappropriate behaviour occurred mainly in the hall and playground, especially when toys or equipment were being used. He usually kicked or smacked a child who had the toy he wanted. He seemed to be unaware that he caused the other child distress and would take the toy away to play with. His play was usually solitary.

Date(s) of assessment(s) _None yet done_

Assessment(s) used _____

Findings of assessment(s):

Action taken:

Key worker allocated to Joe to support him during play sessions and help him achieve specific Stepping stones from the Foundation stage curriculum (see Joe's Small steps planning form)

Have the parents been consulted? Yes/~~No~~   Parent's signature _Flo Bloggs_

Has the SENCO been consulted? Yes/~~No~~ (told but not yet involved)

Signed _Lucinda Handes_   Position _Nursery Nurse_

Date _20 February 2003_   Date review due _20 May 2003_

Small Steps Planning Form

Child's name _____ Area of concern _____

Area of learning _____

Stepping Stone/Early Learning Goal (delete as appropriate):

Small steps to target:	Date achieved	Date checked
1.		
2.		
3.		
4.		
5.		
6.		

Equipment and materials:

Staff involved:

Home support/follow-up:

Small Steps Planning Form

Child's name _Soozie Bubble_ _____ Area of concern _Self-help skills_ _____

Area of learning _Personal, social and emotional development_ _____

~~Stepping Stone~~/Early Learning Goal (delete as appropriate):

Dress and undress independently and manage their own personal hygiene

Small steps to target:	Date achieved	Date checked
1. Soozie will play with the button matching game together with a helper. She will fasten and unfasten the final button in the game, after the helper has shown her how to fasten the others.	13.2.03	17.2.03
2. Soozie will fasten and unfasten the last button when dressing up in the Home Corner, after the helper has done the other buttons.	17.2.03	20.2.03
3. Soozie will fasten and unfasten the last two buttons of her coat each time she puts it on or takes it off, after a helper has done the other buttons.	21.2.03	24.2.03
4. Soozie will fasten and unfasten half of her buttons when dressing and undressing, after the helper has done the other buttons.	27.2.03	
5. Soozie will fasten and unfasten all her buttons independently when dressing and undressing.		
6. Soozie will fasten and unfasten buttons on dolls' clothes, or help other children to dress and undress.		

Equipment and materials:

Button matching game; Soozie's clothes; button-fastening game; dressing-up clothes

Staff involved:

Lucinda Handes and Paula Hardy (daily sessions); Lucy Stevens (Sixth Form work experience, once per week)

Home support/follow-up:

We have asked Soozie's Mum to dress Soozie in clothes that are easier for her to manage than the dungarees, while we work on the buttons in her other garments (coat and cardigans etc.). Soozie takes home the button matching game to play with over the weekends.

PART 3

Early Years Action

Early Years Action is the first formalised level of the revised *SEN Code of Practice* and its main feature is the planning, writing and implementation of an Individual Education Plan (IEP) for the child, practitioner and parents to work with. These are planned by the early years practitioner(s), the child's parents and, if possible and appropriate, with the child's input as well. The plan of action that makes up the IEP should be recorded on an IEP form. The IEP is planned to make sure that the child's difficulties are targeted, and a differentiated programme of work is designed to help the child achieve success in accessing the early years curriculum. A very important part of the planning is that the child's strengths and achievements are recognised and then used as the starting block for moving forward.

The IEP should be constantly monitored and then reviewed at least once per term, more often if necessary. An IEP is a working document and if it appears to be failing the child in any way, it should be reviewed and changed. When the IEP is reviewed, the child's parents and the early years practitioner, with the child if possible, should meet to discuss how and whether the plan needs to be changed. This discussion and the outcome or decisions should be recorded on a review form.

How are the child's difficulties identified at Early Years Action?

You should suspect that the child continues to be experiencing difficulties when they:

- *make little or no progress, even when the setting has used approaches that have targeted the difficulties;*
  In other words, even after you have differentiated the child's work within the usual early years curriculum, the child is still not achieving their targets, or is struggling to achieve them.

- *continue to work at a level significantly below that expected of a child of that age, in certain areas;*
  So, if the child is obviously still struggling to learn things that the other children can achieve relatively easily, you know they are experiencing difficulties. In this situation, identify which area(s) the child finds difficult, make observations of what is happening and record this.

- *display persistent emotional and/or behavioural difficulties despite behavioural management and/or modification strategies that may have been used;*
  Speak to the child's parents and try to find out whether they have noticed the child displaying the same behaviour patterns at home. When you are planning the IEP, perhaps the parents can suggest other strategies for you to try.

- *have sensory or physical problems and make little or no progress despite having the support of personal aids or equipment;*
  This will soon become obvious and you need to take action fairly quickly to make sure that you address the problems while the child is still young.

- *have communication and/or interaction difficulties and need specific support in order to learn;*
  If you think the child is continuing to have problems in this area, check whether they have more difficulties with receptive language than with expressive language. It is easy to assume that a child with an apparently high standard of expressive language does not have difficulties – be wary of falling into that trap.

What happens next?

After identifying a problem, there are several steps you should take:

- *Discuss with the child's parents that you'd like to involve the setting's Special Educational Needs Coordinator (SENCO).*
  When you speak to the parents, stress that you are wanting to make sure their child achieves success in the setting and that speaking with the SENCO is a safety net for the child's good. If your setting has an SEN policy in place, the parents will already know who the SENCO is.
     It is important to be aware that some parents may feel anxious, particularly if you have only just identified the problem and/or if they have had a bad experience of 'professionals' in the past. Some parents may have SEN themselves and have been alienated because of going through a less than happy school system as children.
- *Provide the SENCO with as much information as possible.*
  Give the SENCO your observation records, Foundation stage profile, any assessment results and even examples of the child's work if they illustrate a point you are trying to make.
- *Ask the parents about any other problems such as health difficulties.*
  It can sometimes amaze you that when you talk to the parents an occasional throwaway comment they make gives you a clue about something that could be at the source of a difficulty or tells how to tackle the problem within the setting; or they can suggest a way forward that would work with their child.
- *Liaise with the child's parents, the SENCO and the child to plan and implement the child's IEP. (See 'Planning Individual Education Plans' [IEPs] below).*
  Starting off well at this point is crucial. None of you knows whether it is the beginning of a longer process leading towards a statutory assessment, possibly resulting in the issue of a Statement of Special Educational Needs for the child. Avoid any early hiccups or problems that may cause the parents and/or the child anxiety, worry or even alienation. By being supportive as well as open and honest, you will go a long way to making sure that the process is regarded positively by everybody in the team, especially the child. Active involvement in the planning by the parents and the child means ownership of and commitment to the IEP, and for this reason it is more likely to be successful.

While all this is going on, the SENCO also has some responsibilities. These are to:

- *Make sure the child's parents know about the LEA's Parent Partnership Service (PPS).*
  It is very important for the parents to have all the available information from the LEA. If the parents do not speak English as their first language, the SENCO should make sure they can access the translation services offered by the LEA's Parent Partnership Service.
- *Collect all known information about the child within the setting.*
  This may involve liaising with several professionals to build up a full picture of the child. The SENCO should not consult or involve volunteers or helpers, particularly if they are non-professionals, who come to work in the setting, during this information-gathering

process. Their contribution can only be anecdotal and will not be required, neither will it have any legal standing. Above all, the child's rights of confidentiality must be respected and protected and volunteers must not be given access to private information regarding the child's difficulties.

- *Liaise with outside agents, collecting any relevant information from them.*
  At Early Years Action there may or may not be external professionals involved. If there are, they could be, for example, a social worker or the health visitor. The SENCO should work closely with the outside professional(s) to exchange information and ideas. The parents must be informed of this liaison and if they are not present at any of the meetings, they should be informed of what was said. If there is a written record of a meeting which the parents did not attend, a copy of this should be given to the parents.

- *Liaise with the educational psychologist (EP), if appropriate.*
  At Early Years Action, this may be only on a 'need to know' basis. If the SENCO does make contact with the educational psychologist, this *must* be done with the knowledge and consent of the parents. If the parents are anxious about it, the SENCO should handle the situation with great sensitivity.

- *Decide with the practitioner and parents on the action to be taken and log this onto the IEP.*
  This is discussed in more detail in 'Planning Individual Education Plans' below.

- *Arrange a review meeting at least once every three months.*
  The *Code* suggests that a review should be held at least every three months but, for an early years child, you may need to do this more often, every six weeks or so, depending on the situation. It is a useful idea to book the next review in advance and the child's parents, together with the child if appropriate, should be part of this review process. For more details about holding reviews, see the section 'Reviewing Individual Education Plans' below.

Planning Individual Education Plans (IEPs)

The *Code of Practice* offers some guidance on the planning of IEPs, but this can only be in general terms because each child is unique and therefore the IEP is unique. There is no short cut to planning IEPs by using resources such as software programs that 'write' IEPs and promise you savings of time and effort. It is rare that two children with the same difficulties will achieve success using the same IEP. Children bring to the learning situation their unique experiences, attitudes, backgrounds, styles and so on, none of which can be conveniently fitted into a 'one size fits all' IEP produced on a computer. It is only by working with the child and the parents that you will produce a plan of action that is truly tailored to address that child's difficulties and that will help them to achieve success.

The fine-tuning of the IEP is, therefore, very much an individualised thing (there's a good reason why it's called an *Individual* Education Plan) but there are some general aspects to the planning that can be applied to any child.

- *Focus on a maximum of three or four targets.*
  Any more than this can be overload, which in turn causes more problems for both the child and the practitioner. Since the *Code* says a *maximum* of three or four targets, there is flexibility here to choose only as many as the child can manage, and if this means only one or two, then plan for only one or two. An analogy of this is the speed limit on the motorway – you don't *have* to drive at the maximum of 70 miles per hour; it's fine if you feel comfortable travelling at that speed, but nobody is obliging you to put your foot down on the accelerator and speed along without being confident in doing so. If you do

plan for only one or two targets, make a note about this on the IEP as a record of your professional judgement.

Select the targets according to the child's needs and achievement level, and where possible, link them in with the relevant Stepping Stones or Early Learning Goals of the Foundation stage curriculum, or the targets of the National Curriculum. Always choose the targets from the point that the child has already reached and has experienced success with.

- ~~*The targets should be SMART: Specific, Measurable, Achievable, Relevant and Time-bound.*~~[1]

- *Involve the parents and, if appropriate, the child as well.*
  As we have already discussed, this 'ownership' and involvement gives the parents and the child an incentive to make the IEP work. The age of the child isn't important since even very young children can be involved at an appropriate level. For example, their part could be something like choosing from selected equipment or deciding from several options of activity. Knowing the child and using your judgement here will help the child to become involved.

  Parents should be involved at the planning stage because they have 'inside information' about their child's learning experiences, styles and attitudes. Their involvement at the implementation stage can be in terms of doing follow-up activities and games at home, to reinforce the teaching point. You can work with them to develop a Play Plan which links in with the IEP, and which gives them ideas for supporting the child at home.

Case study

William has Down's Syndrome and some accompanying learning difficulties. He is currently working towards identifying colours, particularly red and blue (other colours will be added later). His Mum and early years practitioner developed a Play Plan aimed at getting William to recognise and name the two colours correctly whenever he was asked. The first part of the Play Plan states what William's targets are and how his Mum will help him work towards them. The second section is for William's Mum to make a record of his progress.

You will find a photocopiable blank version of the Play Plan record form on page 42 and William's Play Plan for one week on page 43.

- *Write the targets concisely, avoiding jargon and flowery language.*
  This makes it easier for everybody concerned. The term used in the *Code of Practice* is 'crisp', a word which captures very well the essence of outlining the targets.

- *Decide on the criteria for success.*
  In other words, how everybody will know when the child has achieved the target. For example, if Daniel is learning to identify his name from among three name cards, you might decide that the criterion for success is correct identification of Daniel's name card three out of four times per check over a period of three days, checked five times per day. Make these criteria achievable for the child, however, because setting them too high will result in immediate failure and therefore immediate lowering of self-esteem, confidence and motivation. There is always room to make the criteria tougher if the child achieves them too easily.

- *Decide on methods of acknowledging and celebrating success, involving the child in your choice.*
  Use careful judgement here as the 'rewards' must be meaningful for the child, and allowing them to choose their credit system will give it currency, since it will be what they actually want. They might, for example, like putting their own stickers on a chart; or maybe they would prefer to be allowed an extra session at the computer; or being able to choose any activity they want gives some children a real buzz.

Be very careful though of using a 'play' session as a reward, since this may create in the child's mind a distinction between 'work' and 'play', which is the last thing you want.

- *Record details of the dates that the child's performance was checked, by whom and with what result.*
  These details are very important and may be crucial at a later stage. Over a period of time they build up to give an overall picture of the child's progress in terms of time, personnel and achievement level.

- *Celebrate the child's strengths.*
  This is vital. It is easy to get bogged down in what Johnny can't do. But there will be many things that Johnny *can* do, and do well, so your first job is to identify the skills he has and work from there. Having recognition of a skill, especially in front of the other children, helps to boost the child's self-esteem and confidence. They will be much more inclined to have a go at something that they perceive as a bit of a challenge.

- *Make a note of which areas are giving difficulty.*
  You also need to be aware of which areas of need you intend to be focusing on. This does not mean a long list of what Fred cannot do, but a brief description of where the problem lies. For example, 'Fred has difficulty in identifying environmental sounds' or 'Fred finds social activities difficult to cope with in large groups'.

- *Be aware of the records of results and whether there is a pattern emerging.*
  As discussed in the section on emotional and behavioural difficulties in Part 2, this pattern might show up problems in the areas of time, place, person or any combination of these. When you have identified where a problem lies, change the element that seems to be the cause.

- *The Code recommends that progress is reviewed every three months, but the IEP can be changed at any time.*
  It is important to keep an eye on the child during the period between reviews in case the IEP is not addressing the child's needs. It isn't written in tablets of stone and if you think you have made a misjudgement in the planning, it's crucial that you act immediately without waiting for the whole of the three-month period. Discuss your concerns with parents and other staff involved, and change the IEP.

- *The teaching methods play a crucial part in the success of an IEP. If a method is not working, then change it.*
  Again, this goes back to person, place or time. But it also may the equipment, the strategies or any combination of these.

- *Keep an ongoing check on targets already achieved.*
  Avoid the 'house built on sand' syndrome. By moving a child on to higher level skills before they've consolidated the earlier ones, you will be building up more problems for them. It is crucial that you make regular checks on targets that have already been achieved. Sometimes the child can forget them and may need to be taught them again or revise them.
  The child with SEN needs lots of repetition, practice, concrete examples and even over-learning sometimes. Don't be afraid of 'overkill', as long as you give the child a variety of interesting and stimulating activities that reinforce the target. If the child needs more practice in order to consolidate the point, then you must allow for this, repeating the teaching if necessary.

- *Be flexible.*
  You may have to use quite a few activities to put across a teaching point. This is where your imagination and ingenuity will come into play, but early years practitioners are past masters at this. Being flexible means finding 100 interesting ways of teaching the same skill or aiming for the same target.

- *Admit failure when an IEP is failing the child, and try again with new ideas.*
  This is part of professionalism. As already mentioned, an IEP is not written in tablets of stone. The child isn't in a position to change the situation, so you have to do it for them. Being professional means having the integrity to acknowledge that a plan isn't working, and then to change it. The child is dependent on us to help them to achieve and we have to accept that responsibility. It is more courageous to concede defeat and go back to the drawing board than to steal time from the child through a false sense of pride.

Positive teaching methods are crucial

It states the obvious to say that an unhappy child cannot learn effectively, so they need positive support and active encouragement. Making sure that you interact with the child in a warm way will go a long way to making sure they are indeed happy in the setting.

- *Always be patient.*
  If the child and/or the session is irritating you, then stop the session and take time out to get back on an even keel. Some children know exactly how to wind you up, especially if you're having an 'off' day! Nobody will gain anything by your becoming stressed, so it's wiser to leave the session until everybody is in a calmer frame of mind.

- *Always be consistent in approach.*
  This is very important for a child with SEN. It reduces the likelihood of confusion. It is also useful if you are absent and another practitioner takes over the programme because they will know exactly what to do and how.

- *Always praise the child whenever they achieve success or **make an effort**.*
  Success breeds success. Praise for achievement is crucial, but you must always be truthful, because the child will know if they didn't really achieve a target, even if you're telling them that they did. Remember too to praise them for their effort, even when a target hasn't been achieved.

- *Always refer to failure in a positive way.*
  Try to avoid using negative words of phrases. For example, 'That was a really good try, Simon. Now let's see if we can crack it by trying it like this' is much more positive in tone than 'Oh, Simon, what a shame you didn't manage it. Maybe next time you'll be better at it.'

- *Always remember: **the child is not here for the professional – the professional is here for the child**.*
  This should be the mantra for all practitioners working with children, at whatever level. It is self-explanatory, but it's something that we need to keep in focus at every stage of planning and putting into practice the child's programme. Working with children with SEN can be very demanding and very tiring, but it can also be very uplifting and can bring immense professional satisfaction as well as pleasure.

The IEP form

LEAs have their own IEP *pro formas* which have on them sections for required information, as outlined in the *Code of Practice*. The obvious things like the child's name and date of birth should be recorded. Even though it seems a simple thing, this is important, especially if the child's name is fairly common or duplicated in the setting.

The form should also record the date it was implemented and the level of the *Code of Practice* such as Early Years Action or Early Years Action Plus. There needs to be a section for the child's areas of strength. It's important to list these because you can easily be distracted by what the child finds difficulty in doing. Because the IEP is going to work from the child's points of strength you need to make a note of what are their abilities and what achievements they have made.

There should be a brief description of the child's areas of difficulty, without making a long list of what Walter cannot do. For example, 'Walter has problems with self-help skills, particularly using the toilet' or 'Walter finds it difficult to turn-take during conversations and his communication skills need to be developed'. This gives some idea to everybody involved what areas they need to focus on.

The listed targets will have a projected achievement date, together with a statement of the criteria for success and the teaching methods (see discussion above). Other necessary information includes which staff will be involved, the frequency of programme, the equipment, apparatus and resources to be used and the date of next review, always remembering that this can be brought forward if you think something needs to be changed sooner rather than later.

You will find a photocopiable IEP form on page 44 and an example of a completed IEP form on page 45.

Reviewing Individual Education Plans

The secret of successful reviews is planning ahead and organisation, with the aid of a shared but confidential calendar or diary in the setting. It is worthwhile establishing a routine for the termly reviews that are held during the earlier levels of SEN provision, with a simple schedule.

There are some practical and useful ideas to follow when planning a review:

- *Set up a system of trigger-reminders in your diary, working backwards from the review date.* Begin to plan about four weeks before review date and jot down a note on each appropriate date, for the things you need to gather together or to do. For example:

12.03.03 (i.e. four weeks ahead) *John Smith's review due on 9.04.03 – request information and advice from:*
John's parents and John
Mrs Davies (early years teacher)
Mrs James (nursery nurse)
Mr McFadden (educational psychologist)
Advice to be received by 26.03.02

22.03.02 (i.e. two and a half weeks ahead) *Advice received so far from*
Mrs Davies
Mrs James
Remind Mr and Mrs Smith and Mr McFadden that advice is due by 26.03.03

26.03.03 (i.e. two weeks ahead) *Send invitations + advice documentation for John Smith's review*

8.04.03 (i.e. the day before) *Get coffee, biscuits and flowers for John Smith's review*

9.04.03 *John Smith's review: 10.00 a.m.*

- *Make the room cheerful and welcoming.*
  You can work magic with coffee and biscuits and some flowers on the table. If possible, invite the parents to come a few minutes earlier to help them relax and collect their thoughts. If English is not their first language they may need an interpreter, so don't forget to arrange one.

- *Arrange chairs in a circle, with a low table in the middle (preferably with flowers on!).*
  This reduces the 'them and us' feel, and emphasises the team approach, that everybody is equal. Some parents may feel extremely threatened or intimidated by the review and they would not feel any easier by walking into a room laid out as if for a formal interview.

- *Refer to the Review Form and work your way through it systematically.*
  This helps to keep everybody focused on each point as it comes up for discussion. It helps you as the Chair to bring people back to the focus point when they start to digress.

- *Invite the main nursery professional for their input.*
  This is crucial as s/he is the practitioner who knows the child most intimately within the setting. S/he will have an overview of the child's performance and progress and also of their attitude to the IEP, their learning style and their overall opinion of what goes on within the setting.

- *Invite the other agents for their contribution.*
  This will usually be at the Early Years Action Plus level, when outside specialists have become involved. But even at Early Years Action, there may be other people who are involved, such as a social worker or a health visitor.

- *Ensure that the child's parents (and the child if appropriate) have an opportunity to express their opinion.*
  It is vital that they feel confident enough to make a contribution and that they are not intimidated. You can design a Parent's Review Form to give to the parents some time before the review and which helps them to focus on the sort of things they could say in the meeting. You will find a blank photocopiable Parent's Review Form on page 48 and an example of a completed Parent's Review Form on page 49.
  If the child is not there in person, and is able to make a contribution to the discussion, this can be done through the parents on a Child's Review Form (see below).

- *Conduct the review so that everybody has time to express their opinion.*
  Watch out for those people who are making a personal bid for an Oscar nomination! Sometimes there are people who tend to hog the limelight and who can take up large amounts of precious time, talking about points that are possibly not very relevant to the review. If you are chairing the review, you can cut in to bring the focus point back under discussion and give the other people present at the review a chance to have their say.

- *Include a plan of further action.*
  This is important so that the meeting can break up and everybody knows the way forward. On the review form, this can be cut down to a simple Yes/No deletion exercise.

- *Before concluding, briefly summarise what was said and what action was decided upon. Ask whether everybody agrees with your summary.*
  It is better to clear up any misunderstandings or misinterpretations immediately than to wait until after the meeting has broken up and find out when it's too late that something was recorded in writing that is incorrect. As an extra precaution, you might like to ask everybody to initial your notes before they leave.

- *Book the date of the next review.*
  People's diaries get filled up very quickly, especially if they are external specialists who visit your setting only occasionally. While everybody is there under your roof, get them to coordinate their dates so that the next review is set.

- *Sign and date the Review Form. If possible, give the parents a copy immediately, otherwise as soon as possible.*

- *Try to have a quiet word with the parents to make sure they are happy with the outcome of the review.*
  This is especially important for parents who are shy, or who feel upset or threatened by the whole thing. They may need to have some of the paperwork explained to them, especially if they have language and/or literacy difficulties themselves. Make sure you do this sensitively and in a supportive way.

- *Have copies of the Review Form made and circulated to all who attended the review as soon as possible.*
  While the meeting is still fresh in the minds of everybody who was there, it is useful to get the paperwork to them. If there are any queries, they can be clarified more or less straight away.

You will find a blank photocopiable review form on page 46 and an example of a completed review form on page 54. From the completed example, you will notice that John is still having difficulties making progress and so the team has decided that he needs to move on to Early Years Action Plus, and that the SENCO will request some additional support from outside specialists.

The child's involvement

A constant theme running through the *Code of Practice* is the involvement of the child where possible. Obviously, there will be some children whose difficulties are so profound that they are unable to take an active part in their SEN provision, but wherever it is possible, at whatever level, it is important that the child is actively a part of the process.

One way of involving the child with their termly (and Annual) review is to provide the parents with a Child's Review Form, and encourage them to record on it what the child says or thinks about the IEP, their progress and so on. Talk the form through with the parents and make sure they are happy about completing it.

You will find a blank photocopiable Child's Review Form on page 50 and an example of a completed Child's Review Form on page 51.

Conclusion

The main points explored in this chapter on Early Years Action are:

- How the child's difficulties are identified.
- What happens after a problem has been identified.
- What are the roles and responsibilities of the practitioner and the SENCO.
- Some practicalities involved in planning Individual Education Plans.
- Involving parents through negotiating Play Plans for them to follow at home.
- Some practicalities involved in reviewing Individual Education Plans.
- Making sure that the child's input is considered when reviewing their IEP.

References

1. *SEN Toolkit*, DfES, 2001.

Play Plan

Play Plan for _____ and _____

_____ will play the games to help _____

_____

Begin by

Here's what _____ did:

Date when this Play Plan was finished at home _____

Play Plan

Play Plan for _William Brown_____ and _William's Mum_____

_____William_____ will play the games to help _William to recognise red and blue_

_and to say their names_____

Sorting and naming all the red clothes he can find, followed by blue things when he knows red very well.
Finger painting using red first, then blue when he knows red.
Sorting and matching all the red shapes, then the blue ones
Naming red things that he takes out of the feely bag; then the blue ones

Begin by

looking at lots of red things (never mind about blue at first); help William to sort out all his red clothes (socks, jumpers, hat etc); say the word 'red' each time and encourage William to repeat it. Then ask 'What colour is this?' – if William needs to be reminded, say 'red' again.

Here's what ____William_____ did:

Monday 5 June. William seemed to mix up the colour with the clothes at first – he'd say Sock when I asked what colour it was, but then he'd say Red after I said it.

Tuesday 6 June. William spotted his dad's red football shirt and shouted Red.

Thursday 8 June. We started looking at blue today. I think he's getting the hang of it. He pointed to my mug and said Blue. His older brother's helping him too.

Saturday 10 June. William can tell you red or blue correctly almost every time you ask, no matter what you point to. I think he's ready to move on to the next colours.

Date when this Play Plan was finished at home _Sunday 11 June_____

Individual Education Plan

Child's name _____ Date of Birth _____

Date IEP implemented _____ Code of Practice level _____

Areas of strength:

Areas of difficulty:

Criteria for success:

1.

2.

3.

Targets to be reached by (date) _____ :

1.

2.

3.

Teaching methods:

Staff involved:

Frequency of programme:

Equipment/apparatus:

Date of next review: _____

**Individual
Education
Plan**

Child's name _John Smith_____ Date of Birth _31.3.2000_____

Date IEP implemented _10.1.03_____ Code of Practice level _EY Action_____

Areas of strength:

John enjoys stories; he can make excellent models.

Areas of difficulty:

John has difficulty with early number work. He has a squint and wears glasses; he regularly attends the eye department at the hospital.

Criteria for success:

1. John will count from 1 to 3 using four different types apparatus, 4 times out of 5.

2. John will recognise and name 1, 2 or 3 when shown in written form in a variety of places, 4 times out of 5.

3. John will correctly write a requested numeral from 1 to 3, 4 times out of 5.

Targets to be reached by (date) _8.4.03_____ :

1. John will be able to count from 1 to 3 using apparatus.

2. John will be able to recognise and name 1 to 3 when shown in written form.

3. John will be able to write any numeral from 1 to 3 on request.

Teaching methods:

Initially in a one-to-one situation in the quiet corner; eventually moving into the main nursery areas to utilise counting displays, posters, name tags and so on.

Staff involved:

Mrs Davies, early years teacher; Mrs James, nursery nurse; Mrs Smith, mother, to work at home.

Frequency of programme:

Twice daily (morning and afternoon) for a maximum of ten minutes, five days per week; once per evening at home when possible.

Equipment/apparatus:

Cubes, counters, plastic sorting shapes, any appropriate counting apparatus of John's choice, paper, pencils and felt-tip pens.

Date of next review: _9.4.03_____

To be attended by Mrs Davies, Mrs Smith and Mrs James

IEP/ Special Needs Termly Review Form

Child's name _____ Date of Birth _____

Level: Early Years Action/Early Years Action Plus (delete as appropriate)

Date of review _____ 1st/2nd/3rd review (delete as appropriate)

Present at review:

Reports of child's progress/IEP:

Additional comments/reports from people not present:

a)

b)

c)

Further action:

Continue with IEP?	Yes/No
Modify IEP?	Yes/No
Remain at present stage?	Yes/No
Move to next stage?	Yes/No
Discontinue SEN procedure?	Yes/No
Other action?	Yes/No

Next review due _____

Name _____ Signed _____

**IEP/
Special
Needs
Termly
Review
Form**

Child's name John Smith _____ Date of Birth 31.3.2000 _____

Level: Early Years Action/~~Early Years Action Plus~~ (delete as appropriate)

Date of review 9.4.03 _____ ~~1st/2nd~~/3rd review (delete as appropriate)

Present at review:

Mr & Mrs Smith (parents); Mrs Davies (teacher); Mrs Cummins (SENCO)

Reports of child's progress/IEP:

1) John can count two items of a variety of apparatus correctly; he still needs to count from 1.

2) John can recognise and name 1 when shown in written form in a variety of places

3) John can write 1 when asked.

The targets have still to be achieved and the criteria need to be reduced. John continues to have difficulties both at home and in the setting.

Additional comments/reports from people not present:

a) Mrs Smith reported on John's opinion. (See attached Child's Review Form.)

John has been happier since the IEP was put in place and he enjoys doing his activities. He says it is hard though and he thinks that his targets are too difficult because he can't remember his work from the day before.

b) Mrs James (Nursery Nurse) reports that John concentrates well but has difficulty in retaining the concept for longer than a few minutes. (See attached detailed report.)

c)

Further action:

Adjust Targets to learn numbers 1–2. SENCO to request input from Early Years Learning Support Service.

Continue with IEP?	Yes/~~No~~
Modify IEP?	Yes/~~No~~
Remain at present stage?	~~Yes~~/No
Move to next stage?	Yes/~~No~~
Discontinue SEN procedure?	~~Yes~~/No
Other action?	Yes/~~No~~ See 'Further action' above

Next review due 21.5.03 (6 weeks) _____

Name A. Cummins (SENCO) _____ Signed _____

Parent's Review Form

Child's name _____ Date of Birth _____

Your child's health:

Is your child usually healthy?

Do they take any medicines? If so, what are they?

Have these changed within the last two months?

Your child at home:

Does your child have any hobbies?

What does your child enjoy doing at home?

What does your child need help with at home?

Your child in _____ :

Is your child happy to come to our setting?

Are you happy about the way we support your child in the setting?

Are you pleased with your child's progress?

Do you have any worries about your child's IEP? If so, what?

Is there anything you think we need to change? If so, what?

What next for your child?

Are you happy with the targets on your child's IEP?

What do you think your child should learn next?

Do you have any questions to ask at the review?

Child's name _Frankie Hudson_   Date of Birth _31.3.1999_

Your child's health:

Is your child usually healthy?   *Yes, apart from the AD/HD*

Do they take any medicines? If so, what are they?

Ritalin

Have these changed within the last two months?

No

Your child at home:

Does your child have any hobbies?

No, but he helps his grandpa with the racing pigeons

What does your child enjoy doing at home?

Playing with his toy cars

What does your child need help with at home?

To behave properly

Your child in _Allenbanks Nursery School_   :

Is your child happy to come to our setting?   *Sometimes*

Are you happy about the way we support your child in the setting?   *Yes*

Are you pleased with your child's progress?   *In some things*

Do you have any worries about your child's IEP? If so, what?

I think he needs to do more work on his behaviour

Is there anything you think we need to change? If so, what?

I think his targets should be easier because he still doesn't behave like we'd hoped

What next for your child?

Are you happy with the targets on your child's IEP?

Yes, I think it's important to concentrate on his behaviour

What do you think your child should learn next?

More concentration. I think he needs to learn to read now

Do you have any questions to ask at the review?

Who are you going to contact about Frankie? Will we be able to join in?
Will he have to leave Allenbanks? I don't want him going to a special school

Child's Review Form

My name is _____

I was born on _____

I like _____

_____

_____

_____

_____

I worry about _____

_____

_____

_____

I still need help with _____

_____

_____

_____

For my next IEP, I want to _____

_____

_____

_____

Parent's signature _____

Date _____

My name is _Gita Kaur_

I was born on _12 September 1998_

I like ~~I like drawing and painting. I like to do jigsaws and make models. I like to~~ dress up in the home corner.

I worry about _number work and reading. Sometimes David Murray teases me._

I still need help with _doing my sums and reading my books._

For my next IEP, I want to _do more games like I play with Mrs James to help me_ with my number work. I want to play the games like letter matching and bingo.

Parent's signature _Pritpal Singh_

Date _19 May 2003_

PART 4

Early Years Action Plus

Early Years Action Plus is the second formalised level of support for the child and is typified by referral to a specialist professional outside of the setting. The *SEN Code of Practice* highlights the importance of the multi-agency approach and the benefits it brings. This collaboration is an important part of supporting the children and their parents, and also provides valuable support to the practitioner who can benefit from a wider spectrum of information and records that focus on different aspects of the child's development. The early years practitioner can take advantage of advice and suggestions about the management of the child's difficulties, such as different teaching strategies, curriculum materials and the organisation of the setting. The *Code of Practice* stresses the importance of everybody involved with the child, including the parents, cooperating closely to ensure seamless provision. There is less risk of misunderstandings and mistakes, and more likelihood of a better quality of provision if liaison takes place on a regular and open basis.

The *Code of Practice* states four important principles for a successful inter-agency partnership:

1. Early identification.
2. Continual engagement with the child and parents.
3. Focused intervention.
4. Dissemination of effective approaches and techniques.[1]

Early identification

Nobody would dispute that early identification of any difficulty is crucial. The old adage 'Catch 'em young' is a very true one, and particularly so when talking about early years children with special needs. For this reason, practitioners are in the front line when it comes to picking up the child who is struggling. Even if they can't identify a specific difficulty, practitioners know from the way the child performs relative to the rest of the peer group that there is something amiss, and are in the best position to call for specialised help early. Time wasted is time lost to these little ones, and the sooner specialised help is put in place, the better.

Continual engagement with the child and parents

This first quarter-century of integration/inclusion of children with special needs has proved that working closely with the parents and the child reaps big rewards. It is true that in the early days, involvement on the part of the parents was often the result of an inspired practitioner rather than a requirement or legislation, but it is now recognised as good practice.

Reduction of anxieties, openness of information, feelings of belonging, a sense of empowerment, possession of the facts, sharing of a commitment, pooling of ideas and suggestions, confidence in knowing what to do and when, willingness to rewrite a failing plan because of joint support. These are benefits shared by everyone in the team, from the child to the outside agent, when a holistic approach is willingly put into practice. The biggest beneficiary is the child, which is the reason everybody is in the game in the first place!

Focused intervention

While the mainstream early years practitioner has the experience and expertise gained from an overview of the wider early years picture, it is probable that they will be less confident in their knowledge of a specialised field. Even practitioners with a special needs qualification are likely to have studied one particular field of difficulty, for example, learning difficulties or communication and language problems, and so would still benefit from cooperating with those outside agents who are specialists in other areas. Referring a child to a specialist agent helps the people involved with the child to sharpen up their approaches to, and perceptions of, the child's difficulties. It helps the practitioners to focus more specifically on methods and strategies that are likely to have a positive outcome for the child's learning and behaviour.

Dissemination of effective approaches and techniques

Something learned is never wasted and practitioners will find that, having used a specialised method with one child, they become more versed in trying similar techniques when they come across another one with difficulties. There is never a guarantee that the same technique will work for two different children, but the practitioner who works closely with the specialist agent is in a position to ask for, try out and expand on many more ways around a problem, than one who tries to move forward unsupported.

There is no room for pride when we are trying to help a small child who is having difficulties. If practitioners don't know the answer, they *must* ask somebody who does, for the child's sake.

Schools in receipt of government funding *must* publish information that includes the arrangements for working in partnership with local education authority support services, health and social services and any relevant local and national voluntary organisations. These details should be included in the Special Educational Needs policy (see Part 1). Private and non-maintained settings ought to consider doing the same, since it helps practitioners to focus on their provision and practices.

Who are the outside agencies?

The term 'outside agencies' means relevant and interested organisations or establishments that are, or could be, involved with the child and the family, to ensure the best quality special needs provision. Among these are:

- The LEA's support services for learning difficulties, speech and language difficulties, visual and hearing impairment and physical disabilities. These support services can provide advice on teaching techniques and strategies, setting management, curriculum materials, curriculum development, direct teaching or practical support for class teachers, part-time specialist help, or access to learning support assistance. Settings should have contact details for these services. If they do not have them, the SEN section of the LEA will be able to supply the relevant details, circulars and information.

- The child or educational psychological services, which can be a very important resource for the early years setting or school. As well as their ability to carry out more specialised assessments, they can suggest problem-solving strategies, including techniques in managing behaviour, and evaluating individual pupil progress. They can also offer information and advice about the development of the SEN policy and help with the professional development of staff in the area of special educational needs, as well as helping with promoting inclusion.

- The behaviour support service.

- Advisers or teachers with knowledge of information technology for children with special educational needs.

- Social services.

- Child protection services.

- Medical services, including health visitors, paediatric nurses and/or paediatricians, nurses, community or hospital-based paediatricians, child psychiatrists, GPs, physiotherapists, speech and language therapists, occupational therapists and hospital-based counsellors. If the child comes to a setting with a condition diagnosed, it is likely that any combination of these outside agents will be involved with the child already. If not, and a difficulty is picked up by the setting, practitioners will probably make contact initially with the local Health Visitor and possibly the child's GP.

- Private and voluntary organisations. There is a plethora of organisations that do some sterling work in their fields and because of their specialised knowledge, they are a valuable source of help and information.

It is possible that some of these agencies are already involved with the child when they enter the early years setting and, even if they remain at the stage of Early Years Action, staff in the setting should work in close partnership with the agents. If the outside agencies are not already involved with the child, and it seems likely that specialist help will be needed when the child moves to Early Years Action Plus, it can be useful to establish positive and cooperative relations with the agencies. Outside specialists can play an important part in the very early identification of special educational needs and in advising the staff in the setting on effective strategies aimed at preventing further special needs developing. They can act as consultants and be a source for in-service advice on learning and behaviour management strategies. As well as these mutual benefits of shared expertise, the liaison and cooperative approach will have become a normal part of the setting's policy on special educational needs long before the agents are called in.

At the Early Years Action Plus level, the Special Educational Needs Coordinator (SENCO) and the child's key practitioner both need to be aware of the availability of the support services and how the setting can access them. Practitioners in maintained settings have an advantage in that LEAs are obliged to provide all the information about their services and how to access them. Voluntary and private settings can establish links with local schools and in this way can also access the information and provision available within the LEA's catchment area.

There are several serious considerations to keep in mind if the setting decides to contract freelance or private specialists or organisations. If it is decided to buy in the expertise of outside professionals, the setting's manager or head must check the qualifications and experience of the agents. They must also make sure that police checks and clearances have been done, and also be aware that the setting rather than the LEA will usually have to pay for this service.

The multi-agency approach should be child-centred and flexible, to make sure that the provision made for the child continues to be appropriate at all times, even when their needs change. It is vitally important that the parents are constantly involved and that information is passed on to them. They may be feeling vulnerable and anxious because of the involvement of another specialist, and they must have the reassurance of openness and honesty on the part of everybody involved, especially the early years setting.

Private or non-maintained settings would be wise to make links with local state-maintained early years providers to share information, facilities, services and best practice. This approach helps to establish a standardised service within the area.

Why call in outside agents?

The early years practitioner(s) and the SENCO have to be very clear why they need the advice and expertise of outside agents. The usual reason is because the practitioners in the setting are not able to offer the expertise needed to manage the child's difficulties. It is the responsibility of the SENCO to make the referral, although before this is done, the practitioner, the child's parents and where possible the child, will have discussed the situation together, and taken a joint decision that this is the plan of action. Even after outside specialists have become involved, the SENCO holds the main responsibility for coordinating the special educational provision made for the child and for any decisions made about this.

Outside specialist support may be needed if the child fulfils one or more of the following criteria as outlined in the *Code of Practice*:

- *The child continues to make little or no progress in specific areas over a long period of time.* The *Code* does not define 'a long period', and it obviously depends on the child, but if there are still concerns after two or three termly reviews (three at the most, which will have given the child a full year) it is crucial not waste any more time.

- *The child continues to work at an early years curriculum substantially below that of the peer group.* This is where careful record-keeping will come into its own. Practitioners will have the Foundation stage profiles plus all the other observations and records as a bank of information that they can use to compare the child's achievement levels with those of the child's peers.

- *The child continues to experience emotional and/or behavioural difficulties that substantially and regularly interfere with the child's own learning or that of the group, despite having an individualised behaviour management programme.* This is particularly important to request specialised support when the IEP seems to be have failed the child. If there is little or no reduction in unwanted behaviours then the practitioners should not waste any more time, since early intervention is crucial.

- *The child has sensory or physical needs, requires specialist equipment and/or requires regular support or advice from specialist practitioners.* This is fairly self-explanatory since it is unlikely that the average early years setting will have the resources to supply the specialist equipment needed by the child.

- *The child continues to have communication and interaction difficulties that impede the development of social relationships and cause problems with learning.* Because communication is at the hub of everything we do, the child who is having problems in this area needs to be identified and supported as soon as possible. If the practitioners are worried, they should ask for help.

Case studies

Rachel, aged four, has attended her day nursery since she was a baby. She seemed to be passing the usual developmental milestones until about 12 months ago. Practitioners have noticed that she is reluctant to play on outdoor equipment such as tricycles, the slide or the climbing frame. When she is outside, she prefers to just run around or sit and watch the others. Some indoor activities seem to cause Rachel difficulties, particularly those that require fine motor skills such as threading, weaving and pegboards. She also has difficulties using bats, balls and beanbags.

Rachel's Mum and the staff planned some IEPs to help Rachel's motor development, and she has been following her programme for eight months. However, recently she has started to have problems at snack and mealtimes, finding it difficult to use her cutlery, or even to hold her beaker for drinks.

At Rachel's latest review it has been decided to refer Rachel to the nursery's health visitor, with a view to getting some specialised help, such as advice offered by the local physiotherapy service, or even a physical assessment to establish whether Rachel has an underlying motor problem.

Daniel, aged five and a half, is due to transfer to Year 1 in three months' time. His Reception class teacher and the LSA are concerned that he will experience difficulties in following the early Key Stage 1 curriculum. The majority of his peer group is working at the level expected of children at that age, but Daniel seems to be achieving at a level markedly lower than the others. In all areas of the Foundation stage curriculum, Daniel is working on the early Stepping Stones, and the Early Learning Goals are some way off yet. Daniel's teacher and LSA have differentiated his work, and implemented IEPs for two terms, but he is still making very little progress. At the next review meeting, Daniel's Mum, the teacher, the LSA and the SENCO decide to refer Daniel to the authority's Learning Support Service, with a view to giving him more appropriate support prior to his move into Year 1.

Pasqual, aged four, entered the early years setting six months ago and within minutes began to show signs of behavioural difficulties. He becomes extremely aggressive towards the other children and will physically assault them if he feels they have upset him. Sometimes there seems to be no apparent reason for his attacks. He finds great difficulty in concentrating on an activity for longer than a minute, and he will often flit from activity to activity. Pasqual's practitioners worked with his Dad (his mother left the family eight months ago) to plan and put into place an IEP designed to help Pasqual to develop positive behaviour, and to increase his concentration. Recently, there have been more episodes of Pasqual's aggression towards the other children and some of the parents are beginning to complain about his behaviour. The setting called for an early review meeting and it was decided to refer Pasqual to the educational psychologist and the pre-school behaviour support service.

Nathaniel, aged five, entered school six months ago with intermittent hearing difficulties, having had grommets fitted shortly before his admission. The grommets have fallen out once and Nathaniel has had further surgery to replace them. His hearing seemed to improve in the weeks immediately following the replacement of the grommets, but lately he appears to be having difficulty in following what is being said to him. He manages by watching what the other children do first, and then he copies them. The school health visitor agrees with Nathaniel's teacher and his Mum that he may need further help in school. It was decided to refer Nathaniel to the Sensory Impaired Support Service for advice regarding specialist equipment and resources that may be appropriate for the setting, and also to liaise with the ENT consultant who is dealing with Nathaniel at the hospital.

Nadine has recently been diagnosed as having an autistic spectrum disorder. She is four years old and attends a mainstream nursery class. She is unable to communicate with the other children and only with adults by taking their hand and putting it on something she wants. Nadine plays on her own, almost always with jigsaws, although she enjoys watching the television, usually choosing *Thomas the Tank Engine* videos. Occasionally she will have a severe outburst of screaming, accompanied by hand-flapping and with her head shaking from side to side. This usually occurs during a changeover of activity.

Nadine's assessment profile shows that she has made very little progress in the last nine months, despite following IEPs, planned by her practitioners and her parents. At the latest review, everybody felt the best plan of action is to refer Nadine to the authority's Speech and Language Support Service.

How are outside agents called in?

Most Early Years Development and Childcare Partnerships (EYDCPs) have in place a set procedure to follow for making referrals to outside agents. Maintained settings should follow this procedure. Private and voluntary settings could link up with their local early years establishments to find out about the procedure and to take advantage of the advice and support that will be on offer.

Whatever way the process is followed, there are several things the practitioners in the setting should do before actually sending off a referral to the relevant outside specialist:

- The practitioner and the SENCO should hold a review meeting with the child's parents and if possible the child. The outcome of the meeting, i.e. that the child is to be referred to the appropriate external agent, should be recorded on the review form and kept in the child's file. At the meeting, the IEP and the child's progress (or lack of it) should be discussed, the parents' and the child's views should be sought and a decision made if more information is needed for the referral.

- Everybody involved should agree what is to go on referral form. It is a good idea to have several blank copies of the form available at the review meeting and to draft the main points of the referral on the form while everybody is gathered together. As the SENCO is the person who will be writing out the form, it is important that they have all the opinions needed to complete it before the meeting breaks up, and also the agreement of everybody at the meeting.

- After the meeting, the practitioner and the SENCO should collect all the relevant information that the outside agent will need. For example, the IEPs, the review forms, records of observations, any assessments or profile records, any samples of the child's work that serve as a good illustration of the difficulties being experienced and so on. All this may involve liaising with several practitioners to build up a full picture of the child and the difficulties they are experiencing. Practitioners need to be wary of involving volunteers or helpers in this information-gathering process. Their contribution can only be anecdotal and will not be required. It is not advisable to involve them.

- The SENCO should then complete the referral form, and together with all the appropriate records and information, send it to the outside agent involved.

You will find a photocopiable referral form on page 60 and an example of a completed referral form on page 61.

Once the referral has been sent off, the next stage involves having a meeting with the outside agent. It is likely that they will make contact first, to agree a date and time for a meeting. Once again, this should include the key practitioner, the SENCO, the parents and the child, if possible. Depending on the nature of the difficulty and who the outside agent is, there may be a preliminary assessment made of the child. This will be more specialised in nature than those held in the setting and will focus more specifically on the area difficulties the child is experiencing.

At the initial meeting between the specialist, the practitioner, the SENCO and the parents, there will be a chance to draw on the advice and suggestions made by the specialist and to plan a new IEP together with them. The new IEP should incorporate some of the strategies and suggestions made by the specialist. It is very important that the parents and the child have the opportunity to make their contribution to the planning of the IEP. Evidently, they will not be expected to have specialist knowledge in the same way as the agent, but they do have their own expertise to offer. For example, through the intimate knowledge the parents have of their child, they will be able to advise as to whether a proposed method of incentive-and-reward will work; through the child's own self-knowledge they will be able to say whether a target is attractive, whether the rewards are motivating and whether the activities are exciting. All these elements are important ones to consider when planning the new IEP, if it is to work.

Once the new IEP is in place and the programme is under way, the main thrust of its implementation will come from the child, the parents and the key practitioner. Usually the outside specialist will pay regular visits to the setting, to monitor the programme and offer ongoing advice. The frequency of the visits will depend on things such as the specialist's workload, the seriousness of the child's difficulties and the amount of support needed by the staff in the early years setting.

In the meantime, the SENCO's responsibilities continue. The child's parents still need to be completely involved and informed about the child's progress, and while this may actually be done by the key practitioner, the SENCO must make sure it does indeed happen.

If the outside specialist calls into the setting, without a prior appointment, because, for example, they were in the area and decided to pop in, the child's parents must be informed of any discussion that takes place concerning the child.

Any advice and support from external agents that may be available to both the key early years professional and the child's parents should be passed on by the SENCO.

The SENCO has to liaise with the specialist agent(s), the child's early years professional, the child and parents to monitor new IEP, the targets, and the teaching strategies. In this way, they will be in a position to take swift action if it appears that any element of the IEP is failing to support the child. (For more discussion of this, see Part 3, 'Planning Individual Education Plans'.)

The SENCO must also ensure that the IEP is reviewed at least once per term at a meeting which, again, involves everybody concerned, including the child if possible. But it is important to remember that interim meetings can always be called if there is a serious concern that needs to be addressed.

The records of the new IEPs must be kept up to date and carefully maintained. If the child is eventually referred for a statutory assessment, the local education authority will ask the setting for evidence of the differentiated work the practitioners have done with the child. The IEPs will form the main body of this strand of the evidence.

Early years practitioners are equal and important members of the team that works together to support the child. It is extremely important that they remember this. Although they have needed to ask for the help of the specialist(s), they must never feel in any way deskilled or ineffective. The specialists have expertise in the particular field they are working in, and the early years practitioners have expertise in the field of mainstream early years education, with an overview of the fuller picture of how children operate in the mainstream setting. The two sets of expertise and experience complement each other to provide a valuable and wide-ranging bank of expertise which can be exploited for the child's good. The expertise of the child's parents which is added to this should go a long way to ensuring that the holistic approach should work smoothly and positively.

Conclusion

The main points explored in this chapter on 'Early Years Action Plus' are:

- that the main thrust at this level is collaborative with approaches with outside agents;
- that the principles of successful inter-agency work are early identification, continual engagement with the child and parents, focused intervention and dissemination of effective approaches and techniques;
- that 'outside agents' consists of a wide range of specialists in fields such as education, health, the voluntary sector and social services;
- that the new IEPs planned will have in them strategies and techniques suggested by the specialist;
- that the referral process should follow that set out by the local EYDCP, but generally speaking the procedure is standardised, to provide a seamless service.

References

1. *Special Educational Needs Code of Practice*, DfES, 2001, 135.

Referral Form to Outside Agents

Child's name _____ Date of Birth _____

Date of referral _____ Name of setting _____

Name of main practitioner _____

Name of SENCO _____

Areas of concern (tick as appropriate):

- ☐ Personal, social and emotional development
- ☐ Physical development
- ☐ Communication, language and literacy
- ☐ Creative development
- ☐ Mathematical development
- ☐ Knowledge and understanding of the world

Have IEPs been put in place? Yes/No Are copies of IEPs enclosed? Yes/No

If not, please state reason:

If other records/documents are enclosed, please state what:

Has the SENCO been involved? Yes/No

If not, please state reason:

Have the parents/carers been involved? Yes/No

If not, please state reason:

Has the child been involved? Yes/No

If not, please state reason:

Reasons for referral (this should be signed by each practitioner who makes a contribution):

Signature of referring practitioner _____

Position _____

Signature of parent/carer _____

Referral Form to Outside Agents

Child's name ___Frederick Jones___ Date of Birth ___18.4.1999___

Date of referral ___16.7.2003___ Name of setting ___Fairfield Nursery___

Name of main practitioner ___Lucinda Handes___

Name of SENCO ___Angela Cummins___

Areas of concern (tick as appropriate):

- ☑ Personal, social and emotional development
- ☐ Physical development
- ☐ Communication, language and literacy
- ☐ Creative development
- ☐ Mathematical development
- ☐ Knowledge and understanding of the world

Have IEPs been put in place? Yes/~~No~~ Are copies of IEPs enclosed? Yes/~~No~~

If not, please state reason:

If other records/documents are enclosed, please state what:

Examples of Frederick's paintings; Foundation stage profile

Has the SENCO been involved? Yes/~~No~~

If not, please state reason:

Have the parents/carers been involved? ~~Yes~~/No

If not, please state reason: Frederick's parents did not want to be involved with doing the IEPs at home

Has the child been involved? Yes/~~No~~

If not, please state reason:

Reasons for referral (this should be signed by each practitioner who makes a contribution):

Frederick's concentration span is no more than two minutes – he usually finds difficulty in staying on task with any single activity for longer than 45 seconds. His maximum time is when he is playing a computer game. His play is usually solitary and he finds difficulty in managing group situations without becoming aggressive towards one of the other children. IEPs targeting these difficulties have failed to help Frederick develop positive behaviour and we need more specialised advice and support. We are concerned that his paintings and drawings are almost always about fighting.

Signature of referring practitioner ___Angela Cummins___

Position ___SENCO___

Signature of parent/carer ___James Jones___

PART 5

Statutory Assessment

A very small number of children, between one and two per cent, will continue to cause concern because of their lack of progress and/or development. When this happens, the people involved with the child may decide that the best course of action is to refer the child to the LEA for a statutory assessment. There are three main sources of referral: the early years setting, the child's parents or another agency.

Early years settings

Early years settings which are maintained or in receipt of government funding have a statutory right to refer a child for assessment, if the child is four to five years old. At the time of writing, children aged three or under who are in an early years setting or nursery may be referred, but the setting does not have a statutory right to do this. From September 2004 however, the LEA's duties will extend to three-year-olds, and from that date these early years settings will have the statutory rights of referral. Child minders or private nurseries can bring a child to the attention of the LEA, which then decides whether a statutory assessment is required.

Parents

Parents may decide to refer their child for a statutory assessment. In this case the LEA has an obligation to carry out the request, unless a statutory assessment has already been done on the child in the six months before the referral, or unless the LEA feels the assessment is unnecessary having considered all the evidence supplied in support of the referral. Once the referral has been made, the LEA must decide within six weeks whether they will carry out the assessment. The LEA must also inform the child's head teacher if the parents have made a referral. When the practitioners and the parents have been working together through Early Years Action Plus, the referral from the parents is probably one that has been agreed by the team. Sometimes however, the parents may be unhappy about the way the setting has dealt with their child's difficulties and they decide to make the referral independently. When this happens, the LEA must consider the referral and take appropriate action.

Other agencies

Another agency can refer a child for statutory assessment. This is usually done by a professional from health or social services, and usually concerns a child under five who has complex or profound difficulties. The LEA will collect evidence in the same way as for referrals through education professionals.

How is a referral made?

For most children, the referral will be made through their early years setting after the processes of Early Years Action and Early Years Action Plus have been worked through. There is a standard procedure to follow when making a referral and normally this would entail the SENCO first liaising with the educational psychologist (EP) who will advise on completing the forms and gathering together the required documentation.

The referral itself is usually made on the LEA's own form but an example of a typical referral form is on page 70 and an example of a completed form is on page 71.

The referral must be accompanied by several pieces of evidence:

- The parents' views, which will have been recorded on review forms at Early Years Action and Early Years Action Plus, but they may also like to include an additional statement to the information pack.

- The child's views, where possible. Again, these should be available in the review records, but also through involvement of the child in the actual referral process. This is discussed in more detail below – see 'Keeping the child involved'.

- Copies of the IEPs used at Early Years Action and Early Years Action Plus will need to be sent with the referral.

- Evidence of the child's progress is an important part of the package. If records have been carefully kept up to date, and the child's progress has been monitored, then the setting will have to hand this required evidence. Records of achievement in the learning areas of the Foundation stage curriculum will also be relevant here.

- If the setting has other relevant records, and information or advice on health-related matters from people such as the health visitor, the child's GP or the speech and language therapist, these must also accompany the referral.

- The views and reports of the outside agents who were called in at Early Years Action Plus must be included, as well as evidence of their involvement. Ongoing records will be able to show this. The setting also has to show to what extent the practitioners actually followed the advice of the outside agents at Early Years Action Plus.

When all the relevant information has been gathered, and the referral form completed, the whole package should be sent to the LEA, which must decide within six weeks whether it will go ahead with a statutory assessment of the child. When the LEA receives the referral, it is obliged to write to the parents outlining the procedures involved in deciding on an assessment, and also informing them of their rights. They will be advised about the LEA's Parent Partnership Service and asked whether they would like the LEA to consult any other professionals if an assessment goes ahead. Within this six-week period, the child's parents have 29 days to inform the LEA whether they agree or not with the referral going ahead. If they agree with the referral, they don't have to wait for the 29 days to expire, but they can tell the LEA at the beginning that they agree, so enabling the LEA to start the process immediately.

It occasionally happens that the LEA will turn down a request for a statutory assessment and in this case it must write to the child's parents and the setting, giving the reasons for its refusal. The parents have the right to appeal to the SEN Tribunal if they disagree with the LEA's decision. If the LEA's decision is that they will indeed make a statutory assessment of the child, then the next stage of the procedure begins.

What happens next?

Once the LEA decides to make a statutory assessment it has a strict timetable* to adhere to and must complete the process within the following ten weeks, because at that point it has to decide whether to start the next stage, which is the issuing of a Statement of Special Educational Needs.

At the start of the assessment process, the LEA will contact the child's parents, all the professionals involved with the child and the educational psychologist for their opinions and advice regarding the child's current progress.

As practitioners in the early years setting, you have a very important part to play here since you will have the fullest picture of the child's achievements in relation to their peer group and the Foundation stage curriculum. As the professionals who have been involved with the child all the way through the earlier levels, you will know which strategies were successful and which were less effective, how the child performed, what they found difficult and what they achieved. You are also the people who know better than anybody what the child's learning styles are, how they react to certain activities or situations in the setting, and how they interact with the other children in the group.

Completing educational advice

The LEA is likely to have its own set of forms to complete, and it will send these to the setting, with a letter requesting the educational advice. Practitioners doing this for the first time should not feel worried about this, since they will have all the information they need in the child's records. To help focus thoughts, and to bring together some of the information, thinking about the following questions could be helpful:

Communication and language skills

- Is the child's main language English? If not, what language is spoken at home?
- Does the child communicate by speech, gestures, oral sounds or not at all?
- Does the child make eye contact during conversations?
- Is the child's speech clear?
- Does the child always communicate or just sometimes?
- Does the child communicate with adults or the other children or both, or neither?
- Does the child understand what is said to them?
- Does the child talk about everything, or just a few topics, or only one?
- Does the child use the kind of language expected from a child of that age?
- Can the child play imaginatively?

Social, emotional and personal skills

- Does the child interact well with the other children?
- Does the child have difficulties with relationships with the adults in the setting?
- Does the child share and turn-take appropriately?
- Does the child get easily upset over small things?

---

*You will find a useful flow chart of the timetable for making statutory assessments and issuing Statements of Special Educational Needs in the *SEN Code of Practice* on page 120. Spot the spelling mistake at the point where the LEA decides whether to assess the child!

- Does the child play happily with other children? Can the child also play happily alone?
- Does the child have a reasonable concentration span?
- Does the child have any ritualistic or obsessive behaviour? For example, hand-flapping, spinning the wheels on toys, doing the same jigsaw time after time?
- Does the child become distressed at any change in the routine?
- Can the child join in group activities and discussions confidently?
- Has the child developed self-help skills, i.e. are they independent at the toilet, at meals or at dressing?

Physical skills

- Does the child have any physical difficulties?
- Has the child developed gross motor skills, i.e. can they run, jump, climb, kick a ball, ride a tricycle, hop, and skip etc.?
- Has the child developed fine motor skills, i.e. can they manipulate puzzles, do threading or cutting with scissors, use pencils, crayons or paintbrushes, etc.?
- Does the child have good eyesight?
- Is the child's hearing good?

Learning abilities

- Is the child experiencing difficulties in learning? For example, with early literacy skills or early mathematical concepts?
- Does the child need lots of repetition and practice before learning a concept?
- Does the child seem to learn something one day and forget it the next? Does this happen fairly often?
- Can the child predict the next part of a story? Can they solve problems? Can they make simple decisions?
- Does the child show curiosity about how things work? Do they have an interest in the world around them?

Medical and health issues

- Does the child have any known medical condition or disability?
- Does the child have any allergies?
- Does the child have any special dietary needs?
- Does the child need to take medication on a regular basis?
- Does the child have any sensory disability? For example, visual or hearing?
- Does the child have any physical disability?
- Does the child have prolonged absences from the setting for medical reasons?

By answering these questions, and then adding the information about the child that you have in the records, you will soon supply the LEA with the useful and quality educational advice that it needs to help it make a decision about issuing a Statement.

It does not necessarily follow that making a statutory assessment of a child will result in the writing of a Statement of Special Educational Needs. When all the advice has been submitted, the LEA may decide not to proceed any further. In this case, the LEA must write to the child's parents and the setting, explaining the reasons for the decision. As well as giving an explanation for the decision not to go ahead with the assessment, the LEA has to outline what provision it thinks is appropriate to meet the child's needs.

Once again, the parents have the right of appeal to the SEN Tribunal if they disagree with the LEA's decision.

If the LEA does decide to make an assessment of the child's needs and collects all the relevant advice, then the next stage of the process begins. This usually involves the writing and issuing of a Statement of Special Educational Needs, which is a legally binding document outlining the areas of difficulty being experienced by the child, and the most appropriate provision for meeting the child's needs.

Statement of Special Educational Needs

While the LEA will usually write and issue a Statement of Special Educational Needs, it doesn't always do so. If it decides that a Statement is not necessary, after examining all the evidence gathered from the statutory assessment, it has to inform the child's parents within two weeks of the completion of the assessment and the making of the decision.

If, however, the LEA does decide to issue a Statement, it has to send a draft copy of the Statement to the parents within the same time limit of two weeks, and the final Statement must be written and issued within eight weeks from that point. In other words, the entire process from initial referral to Statement must not take any longer than 26 weeks.

Pages 100–101 of the *Code of Practice* give a very clear and useful outline of the required format and information in the Statement. There are six obligatory sections:

1. *Introduction*, giving the child's personal details, i.e. their name, date of birth and address, as well as their parents' names and address(es). It also has the child's home language and religion.

2. *Special Educational Needs (learning difficulties)*, giving the details of every area of difficulty that was identified by the LEA during the assessment. All the advice that was received from everybody involved has to be attached as appendices to the statement.

3. *Special Educational Provision*, giving details of the type of provision that the LEA considers would best meet the needs of the child. This includes:

   a. the objectives that the provision should aim to meet;
   b. the actual SEN provision which is appropriate to meet the needs specified in Part 2 of the Statement;
   c. what arrangements will be made to monitor whether the objectives are being met, whether the child is progressing towards their short-term targets and how their progress will be reviewed on a regular basis.

4. *Placement*, giving the name and type of school or setting where the child will be attending, or if not a named school or setting, how the LEA will make provision for the child.

5. *Non-educational Needs*, giving details of all the relevant non-educational needs of the child, as agreed between the LEA and health professionals, social services or other agencies.

6. *Non-educational Provision*, giving details of the relevant non-educational provision that will meet the non-educational needs of the child, as agreed between the LEA and health professionals, social services or other agencies.

The Statement must have attached five or six important pieces of advice including the parents' evidence, the educational advice, the medical advice, the psychological advice, the social services advice and any other advice such as the child's views, or any other agent whose advice is relevant.

Once the final Statement has been written, a copy of it must be sent to the child's parents together with details of their right to appeal to the SEN Tribunal, if they disagree with anything in the Statement.

Annual/Biannual Review

A Statement of Special Educational Needs must be formally reviewed annually, but if the child is under five, the Statement should be informally reviewed every six months. This is to make sure that the recommendations made in the Statement still apply to the child, and are still the most appropriate way of making sure their needs are being met. The six-monthly review need not be as formal or using the full range of documents as the main, annual review. The *Code of Practice* enables the Statement to be amended if necessary, at the six-monthly review.

Keeping the child involved

An important and recurring theme running through the *Code of Practice* is the importance of the child's involvement at every stage of the process. Even very young children can be involved at an appropriate level, if their difficulties don't prevent them from communicating. There are quite a few ways you can help children in the early years setting to become an integral part of their own planning and decision-making. The biggest advantage in this is the way it helps the child to feel confident and happy about the process they have become a part of. By demystifying it and making it less frightening or threatening, the child's fears and concerns will be dramatically lessened when they become an active member of the team.

Sometimes the child will need the help of their parents or an adult from the setting to express their views and opinions, but this doesn't lessen the importance of what they have to say.

- It is important to develop within the setting an ethos where individual differences are accepted and respected. By having resources and books in the setting that reflect a wide range of abilities, and by regularly sharing these together with all the children, special needs will come to be seen as just another aspect of our society.

- Part of supporting the child in their involvement means talking to them about their difficulties and why they are going through the various stages of assessments, IEPs and reviews etc. As the child's primary practitioner, you will be in the best position to know how to pitch this at the child's level. It's important to use the vocabulary and style of language that the child is familiar with, to make sure they really understand what's going on. For example, if the child knows and uses the term 'adult', then you can refer to the outside agents as 'the adults from a different place who come here to help you', but if the child is more familiar with the term 'grown up', then it would be better to use those words.

- Encourage the child to focus on how they are different and special, by helping them to express how they feel about their own difficulties. Talk about the problems that the child is experiencing and encourage them to tell you how they feel about it.

- Make sure that the child doesn't focus so much on their difficulties that they think there's nothing else to say about themselves except their problem. You can do this by encouraging the child to tell you *everything* about themselves, such as their favourite story, film, television programme, toy, game etc., what makes them laugh, what makes them sad, what their biggest wish is, and so on. You could help the child to make a book about themselves, with photos, pictures and what they have said written inside.

- Encourage the child to tell you about how they see themselves in the setting. Get them to tell you what they are good at, what they enjoy doing, what they have learned, what they find hard to do, what they don't like doing.

- Help the child to understand that the things they need help with developing are their special educational needs. It's helpful to use the phrase from the beginning because the child will hear it a great many times before the process is finished. Explain that it's the adults' way of describing what things the child needs more help with than other children. You can help the child to see what you mean by talking in terms of the child's particular difficulties.

- Talk with the child about the outside agent(s) who have been, or are going to be, involved with them. Explain what the agents' part is in the overall plan and encourage the child to tell you how they feel about this. You could encourage the child to draw or photograph the outside agents and include them in their book about themselves.

- If the child goes on to statutory assessment, help them to understand the process and what it involves. Again, use the correct terminology, explaining that it just means that everybody who works with them will be asked to write what things they are good at, what things they find difficult and what sort of help they need to learn the things they find hard.

- If the child is unsure about who is involved and what role they play in the process, take the time to introduce each member of the team, and what their job will be. This all helps to reassure the child that everybody is working together in their own way, to make sure the child gets the help they need.

- If the child goes on to have a Statement of Special Educational Needs written, explain to them that this is just an important paper written by the education authority and has written on it all the things that should be done to help the child learn the things they find difficult.

- Make sure that there are ways of giving the child extra help that they may not be getting at the moment. These could be things like special equipment such as a wheelchair or a computer, an extra helper in the setting or even going to a different setting. It is important to prepare the child for the type of specialised help they are likely to be allocated. Encourage the child to talk to you about this, about the help they have at the moment and the kind of extra help they would like to have. All of this information will form part of the child's contribution to the statutory assessment and/or the Statement.

If the child is able to make their contribution to the process in this way, it can be useful to record it all on a form that is included with the information gathered together from everybody involved. You will find an example of such a form on page 72 and an example of a completed form on page 73.

There are some excellent books available that will give detailed help about the ways you can make sure the child is involved. Hannah Mortimer's *Taking Part* (QEd, 2000) is a practical and helpful book that gives sound advice for both the practitioner and the child. You can also find guidelines and suggestions in the *SEN Toolkit* (DfES, 2001).

Conclusion

The main points explored in this chapter on statutory assessment are:

- The three main sources of referral for statutory assessment: the setting, the child's parents or another agency.
- How a referral is made and the evidence that must accompany the referral form.
- The timetable that the LEA must follow when the process is set into motion.
- What goes into completing educational advice.
- Making an assessment of the child's special educational needs.
- Writing a Statement of Special Educational Needs.
- Involving the child in the statutory assessment.

Referral Form for Statutory Assessment

Child's full name _____ Date of Birth _____

Home address _____

_____

Home language _____ Religion _____

Parent's/carer's name(s) _____

Address if different from child's _____

Relationship if not parent _____

Parent's/carer's signature _____ Date _____

Name of setting _____

Name of Head/Manager _____

Name of SENCO _____

Name, address, telephone number and position of outside agent(s) involved
and date(s) of initial involvement:

_____

_____

_____

Please tick which of the following documents are enclosed with this referral:

☐ IEPs: Early Years Action and/or   ☐ IEPs: Early Years Action Plus

☐ IEPs Review Forms:
   Early Years Action and/or   ☐ Early Years Action Plus

☐ Foundation stage/
   National Curriculum records   ☐ Other assessment(s)

☐ Setting's report/advice   ☐ Health records

☐ Social service records

Other (please specify) _____

☐ Outside agent(s) reports   ☐ Parents' views

☐ Child's views

Signature of referring practitioner _____

Position _____ Date _____

Referral Form for Statutory Assessment

Child's full name <u>Frankie Hudson</u>   Date of Birth <u>31.3.99</u>

Home address <u>45 Orchard View, Allenbanks, Northumbria, NE99 0CD</u>

Home language <u>English</u>   Religion <u>Christian</u>

Parent's/carer's name(s) <u>Sheena Grainger and David Hudson</u>

Address if different from child's <u>12 Dockside Rd, Allenbanks NE98 4AF</u>

Relationship if not parent _____

Parent's/carer's signature <u>Sheena Grainger</u>   Date <u>14.7.2003</u>

Name of setting <u>Allenbanks Nursery School</u>

Name of Head/Manager <u>Mary Frampton</u>

Name of SENCO <u>Angela Cummins</u>

Name, address, telephone number and position of outside agent(s) involved and date(s) of initial involvement:

James McGuire, Ed Psych, Allenbanks CDC, Tel 0164 332 6510

Simon Peters, GP, Allenbanks Surgery, Tel 0164 332 5027

Clare Daniels, HV, Allenbanks Surgery, Tel 0164 332 5027

Margaret Collins, Behaviour Support Service, Allenbanks CDC, Tel 0164 332 6510

Please tick which of the following documents are enclosed with this referral:

☑ IEPs: Early Years Action and/or   ☑ IEPs: Early Years Action Plus

☑ IEPs Review Forms:
  Early Years Action and/or   ☑ Early Years Action Plus

☑ Foundation stage/
  National Curriculum records   ☐ Other assessment(s)

☑ Setting's report/advice   ☑ Health records

☐ Social service records

Other (please specify) _____

☑ Outside agent(s) reports   ☑ Parents' views

☑ Child's views

Signature of referring practitioner <u>Mary Frampton</u>

Position <u>Head Teacher</u>   Date <u>16.7.2003</u>

Child's Contribution to Statutory Assessment

My name is _____

I was born on _____

I am _____ years and _____ months old

I wrote this form with _____ who is my

_____

I think I have special educational needs because _____

_____

I am good at _____

_____

I find it hard to _____

_____

I like to _____

_____

I don't like to _____

_____

I laugh at _____

_____

I can get sad at _____

_____

This is the extra help I have now _____

_____

I think I will need more extra help such as _____

_____

I would like to have help with _____

_____

I have written my name here _____

Today is _____

Child's Contribution to Statutory Assessment

My name is _Caroline Anne Shepherd_

I was born on _9 January 1998_

I am _____5_____ years and _____4_____ months old

I wrote this form with _Mrs Jones_ who is my

Nursery teacher

I think I have special educational needs because _I can't hear very well and I take longer to learn things than my friends_

I am good at _jigsaws and drawing and making friends_

I find it hard to _hear clearly and do my reading and writing and talking_

I like to _play with my friends and climb on the climbing frame_

I don't like to _do sums and writing_

I laugh at _my Daddy and Jess the cat and Wallace & Grommet_

I can get sad at _when people's dogs die and when I get told off_

This is the extra help I have now _Mrs Cummins works with me every morning and afternoon for fifteen minutes each time_

I think I will need more extra help such as _things to help me to hear better and to speak more clearly_

I would like to have help with _my reading and writing_

I have written my name here _Caroline_

Today is _7 May 2003_

APPENDIX

Example of an early years setting's SEN policy

Fairfield Nursery Special Educational Needs (SEN) Policy

Everyone at Fairfield Nursery believes that all children have a right to a broad and balanced early years curriculum. **We welcome** *all* children, regardless of their individual needs and we aim to welcome them to an inclusive setting. In order to achieve this, we work closely with the children, their parents or carers and other agencies if this is necessary.

We aim to identify any difficulties a child might have and to work with the child and their parents or carers to address those difficulties.

We admit all children living in the Fairfield and Allenbanks Borough, aged 2 years 6 months to school age. Sometimes a child may need extra support in some way – **we encourage** parents who think their child might have particular needs to talk to us about this.

Our special educational needs coordinator or SENCO is called Clare Smith and she:

- helps us to identify any difficulties a child may have;
- helps us to develop our strategies and plans of action;
- keeps parents or carers in touch with their child's progress;
- helps us all to review this SEN policy each year;
- keeps in touch with outside agencies who can help;
- keeps us all up to date on SEN matters.

Staff training in SEN: Anne Jones (Nursery Manager) is also a trained and qualified speech and language therapist. All our staff attend SEN training courses regularly through the Fairfield and Allenbanks Local Education Authority early years professional development programmes.

Our SENCO attends six days SEN training each year and she also meets other SENCOs regularly to share ideas and up-to-date information about SEN.

We have a wide selection of books and pamphlets about SEN and the LEA's support services for parents or carers to borrow – feel free to ask your child's key worker about these. We have regular contact with the area physiotherapist and occupational therapist services.

We monitor this SEN policy by:

- reviewing it with the SENCO each July – parents or carers are invited to contribute their ideas and opinions to the review;
- circulating it to all parents or carers every year;
- asking parents, carers and staff regularly about how well we are meeting SEN in our nursery;
- monitoring the progress which children with SEN are making;
- talking with the children about how they feel about their setting, their IEPs and their play.

We identify SEN through Early Years Action:

- We check each child's progress and monitor any child who seems to be having difficulties in any area of learning, including problems with behaviour.
- We record each child's progress and share it with parents or carers on a regular basis through discussions and/or the home-nursery diary.

- If a child needs something additional to or different from our usual early years curriculum, we discuss this with their parents or carers (and if possible the child) and together prepare an *Individual Education Plan* (IEP) which shows clear targets for the child. We review this plan regularly with parents or carers (and their child if appropriate).
- We discuss with the parents or carers how they can support their child's progress at home.

We ask for further support through Early Years Action Plus:

- If a child is still having difficulties and their needs are not being met within the nursery, we can request further support and advice from the LEA's support professionals such as the early years learning support teacher, the sensory support teacher, the behaviour support teacher, the educational psychologist, the specialist health visitor, the speech and language therapist or the physiotherapist.
- The SENCO will liaise with the external professionals and the child's parents or carers, together with the child if appropriate, in planning a new IEP.
- The SENCO will organise review meetings with external professionals, parents or carers and the key worker to monitor progress.

If the child continues to have difficulties and we feel we cannot meet their needs sufficiently at Fairfield Nursery, the SENCO will consult with parents or carers and external professionals, before requesting the LEA to carry out a statutory assessment.

We plan approaches for children with SEN by:

- differentiating our activities so that all the children can achieve them, and all the children can experience success and gain confidence;
- allocating a key worker to each child with SEN in order to monitor the child's progress and learning;
- ensuring that our planning for all the children contains approaches and activities which help those children who have SEN to make progress;
- adapting our materials and teaching styles to help children with different individual needs to learn.

Our buildings are suitable for wheelchair access and there is a loop system for the deaf and hard of hearing. We have purpose-built toilet and shower facilities for the disabled and also a quiet area. We have a soft-play room and the outdoor play area has been fitted with soft safety paving.

Complaints about our SEN provision: If parents or carers have a complaint about the way we are working with their child who has SEN, they should speak to the key worker initially, and if they are still not happy, they should approach the SENCO. She will look into the problem and report back within a week. If parents or carers continue to be dissatisfied, the SENCO will refer the matter to the Manager to take further action as appropriate.

We meet with parents or carers at least once a term to discuss their child's progress. We also put together an *All About Me* book for parents or carers to share with their child. This shows our approaches and activities that term, with photographs and records of work. We *always* discuss with parents or carers beforehand when we wish to contact another professional about their child, unless there are concerns about Child Protection.

Moving on (transition):

We give the child's progress reports, plans and assessments and records of reviews to the next setting or school when the child leaves Fairfield Nursery. Our SENCO liaises with other settings when the child moves on or if they attend more than one setting at the same time.

Signed _____

Date _____

Further reading

Special Educational Needs Code of Practice, DfES, 2001.

SEN Toolkit, DfES, 2001.

All Together: How to Create Inclusive Services for Disabled Children and their Families. A Practical Handbook for Early Years Workers, M. Dickins and J. Denziloe, National Children's Bureau, 2nd edition, 2003.

Special Needs In Early Years Settings: A Guide for Practitioners, Collette Drifte, David Fulton Publishers, 2001.

Early Learning Goals for Children with Special Needs, Collette Drifte, David Fulton Publishers, 2002.

Effective IEPs Through Circle Time: Practical Solutions to Writing Individual Education Plans for Children with Emotional and Behavioural Difficulties, Margaret Goldthorpe, LDA, 2001.

Right from the Start: Effective Planning and Assessment in the Early Years, Vicky Hutchin, Hodder & Stoughton, 1999.

Special Needs Handbook: Meeting Special Needs in Early Years Settings, Hannah Mortimer, Scholastic, 2002.

Taking Part, Hannah Mortimer, QEd, 2000.

The SEN Code of Practice in Early Years Settings, Hannah Mortimer, QEd, 2002.

Special Needs and Early Years: A Practitioner's Guide, Kate Wall, Paul Chapman Publishing, 2003.

Glossary

ADD – Attention Deficit Disorder.

ADHD – Attention Deficit Hyperactive Disorder.

AIDS – Acquired Immune Deficiency Syndrome.

Allergy – A condition that results in an adverse physical reaction to a substance such as certain foods or synthetic packaging.

Asperger's Syndrome – A communication disorder that falls within the autism range.

Asthma – A condition which affects the respiratory system.

Autistic Spectrum Disorder – A range of language, communication and social disorders.

Cystic fibrosis – A condition mainly affecting the lungs and pancreas, although the liver and sweat glands may also be affected.

DfES – Department for Education and Skills.

DES – Department of Education and Science.

Diabetes – A condition which affects the absorption of sugars and starch in the body.

Down's Syndrome – A chromosomal abnormality which is characterised by recognisable features.

Dyscalulia – A condition causing specific learning difficulties in mathematics.

Dyslexia – A condition causing specific learning difficulties in reading and spelling.

EBD – Emotional and Behavioural Difficulties.

Eczema – A condition which affects the skin.

EP – Educational psychologist.

Epilepsy – A condition of abnormal electrical activity in the brain which results in seizures.

EYDCP – Early Years Development and Childcare Partnership.

EYLSS – Early Years Learning Support Service.

GP – General practitioner.

Haemophilia – A hereditary condition of the blood which can result in severe internal haemorrhaging after only a slight knock.

HIV – Human Immunodeficiency Virus.

HV – Health Visitor.

IEP – Individual Education Plan.

IPSS – Independent Parental Support Service.

LEA – Local education authority.

LSA – Learning Support Assistant.

Makaton – A system of signing, for communicating with people who have communication, language or literacy problems.

MLD – Mild or Moderate Learning Difficulties.

PSS – Parental Support Service.

Semantic-Pragmatic Disorder – A social and language disorder that falls within the autistic spectrum.

SEN – Special Educational Needs.

SENCO – Special Educational Needs Coordinator.

SLD – Specific Learning Difficulties/Speech and Language Difficulties/Severe Learning Difficulties.